The Best General Interest Places on the Internet

> *Some people talk about their interests or things they like; others put up pictures of their families or other favorite images.*

◀ *Although many of the places on the World Wide Web are for business users, thousands of sites have been put up by regular people.*

The World Wide Web is almost exclusively a one-way medium, meaning that you can't respond to people's Web pages like you can in Usenet. However, that too is changing, and some Web sites allow discussion and comment.

The Internet is also a good place to get help in times of need or to find others to talk to. Electronic mail has helped link millions of people who might not have ever met. There are many places on the Internet where you can meet people with like interests, find new friends, and share personal experiences.

▼ *The Web also has many sites that relate to people's interests. Some of these sites have links to other sites, and thus act like catalogs of Internet resources.*

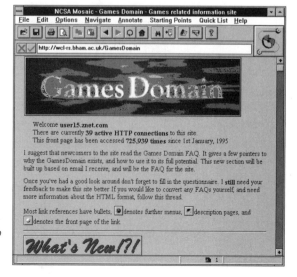

▶ *The Games Domain site lists other Web sites, Usenet news groups, file download sites, and so on, all related to games.*

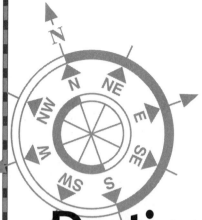

Destination INTERNET
& World Wide Web

by Paul Hoffman

IDG Books Worldwide, Inc.
An International Data Group Company

Foster City, CA ♦ Chicago, IL ♦ Indianapolis, IN ♦ Braintree, MA ♦ Dallas, TX

Destination INTERNET & World Wide Web

Published by
IDG Books Worldwide, Inc.
An International Data Group Company
919 E. Hillsdale Blvd., Suite 400
Foster City, CA 94404

Library of Congress Catalog Card No.: 95-77664

ISBN: 1-56884-469-7

Printed in the United States of America

10 9 8 7 6 5 4 3 2 1

1B/RY/QZ/ZV

Distributed in the United States by IDG Books Worldwide, Inc.

Distributed by Macmillan Canada for Canada; by Computer and Technical Books for the Caribbean Basin; by Contemporanea de Ediciones for Venezuela; by Distribuidora Cuspide for Argentina; by CITEC for Brazil; by Ediciones ZETA S.C.R. Ltda. for Peru; by Editorial Limusa SA for Mexico; by Transworld Publishers Limited in the United Kingdom and Europe; by Al-Maiman Publishers & Distributors for Saudi Arabia; by Simron Pty. Ltd. for South Africa; by IDG Communications (HK) Ltd. for Hong Kong; by Toppan Company Ltd. for Japan; by Addison Wesley Publishing Company for Korea; by Longman Singapore Publishers Ltd. for Singapore, Malaysia, Thailand, and Indonesia; by Unalis Corporation for Taiwan; by WS Computer Publishing Company, Inc. for the Philippines; by WoodsLane Pty. Ltd. for Australia; by WoodsLane Enterprises Ltd. for New Zealand.

For general information on IDG Books Worldwide's books in the U.S., please call our Consumer Customer Service department at 800-762-2974. For reseller information, including discounts and premium sales, please call our Reseller Customer Service department at 800-434-3422.

For information on where to purchase IDG Books Worldwide's books outside the U.S., contact IDG Books Worldwide at 415-655-3021 or fax 415-655-3295.

For information on translations, contact Marc Jeffrey Mikulich, Director, Foreign & Subsidiary Rights, at IDG Books Worldwide, 415-655-3018 or fax 415-655-3295.

For sales inquiries and special prices for bulk quantities, write to the address above or call IDG Books Worldwide at 415-655-3200.

For information on using IDG Books Worldwide's books in the classroom, or ordering examination copies, contact Jim Kelly at 800-434-2086.

For authorization to photocopy items for corporate, personal, or educational use, please contact Copyright Clearance Center, 222 Rosewood Drive, Danvers, MA 01923, or fax 508-750-4470.

is a registered trademark under exclusive license to IDG Books Worldwide, Inc., from International Data Group, Inc.

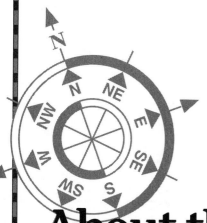

About the Author

Paul Hoffman

Paul E. Hoffman has written more than a dozen computer books, many of them about the Internet (including IDG Books' *The Internet*, the official book of the Public Television presentation "The Internet Show," and *Netscape and the World Wide Web For Dummies)*; in fact, he's been active on the Internet for more than 15 years. As president of Proper Publishing, he now runs his own Internet service, the popular Internet Computer Index site on the World Wide Web. Since 1987, he has been the News Editor at *MicroTimes*, the largest regional computer magazine in the United States.

Acknowledgments

There were so many people involved in the production of this book who deserve mention. I would like to thank several of the folks at IDG Books Worldwide and at Compaq who helped shepherd this book through its many steps: Megg Bonar, Suki Gear, Mary Corder, Mary Bednarek, Beth Jenkins, Cindy Phipps, Drew Moore, Heidi Steele, Diane Steele, Gina Scott, Steve McGuire, Kathy Hanley, David Solomon, Brenda McLaughlin, Eric Stone, and Amy Marks at IDG Books, and David Vining, Patricia Dalheim, and Pat Kubick at Compaq. Thank you, all.

Credits

V.P. and Group Publisher
Brenda McLaughlin

Associate Publisher
Eric Stone

Acquisitions Editor
Megg Bonar

Brand Manager
Pradeepa Siva

Acquisitions Assistant
Suki Gear

Production Director
Beth Jenkins

Supervisor of Project Coordination
Cindy L. Phipps

Supervisor of Page Layout
Kathie S. Schnorr

Pre-Press Coordinator
Steve Peake

Associate Pre-Press Coordinator
Tony Augsburger

Media/Archive Coordinator
Paul Belcastro

Project Editors
Mary C. Corder
Amy Marks

Editors
John Levine
Heidi Steele

Editorial Assistant
Heather Albright

Production Staff
Gina Scott
Carla C. Radzikinas
Patricia R. Reynolds
Melissa D. Buddendeck
Dwight Ramsey
Robert Springer
Leslie Popplewell
Theresa Sánchez-Baker
Drew R. Moore

Proofreader
Kathleen Prata

Indexer
David Heiret

Cover Design
Three 8 Creative Group

Book Design and Layout
Jo Payton

Illustrators
Steve McGuire
Kathy Hanley

Table of Contents

Part 3: Internet Information Services _____ 73

Foreword

Welcome to the fastest growing medium on the planet — and the least predictable, not to mention the hardest to make sense of. A 1950s TV executive would still recognize that medium today, but the Internet's 1960s Pentagon godparents would be astonished to discover that their national security conduit had mutated into a venue for everyone from propellerheads and cyberpunks to librarians and executives, all eagerly exploring this new digital wilderness. It is a world where e-mail is quaintly old-fashioned, and the real action lurks behind an alphabet soup of beckoning jargon. MUDs, MOOs, WWW, M-bone — all mark the edge of this new electronic frontier.

But the Internet's burgeoning unpredictability is more than a curiosity. It is an artifact of the radically decentralized architecture that defines the very soul of the Internet. Its architects took this approach to ensure communications continuity in the event of nuclear war, but the same feature that once protected the warlords' data from Russian bombs now shields infonauts from innovation-killing meddlers. Thus, it is a safe bet that when it comes to generating surprises, the Internet is still in its infancy.

The Internet is nothing less than a wildly mutating communications anarchy, growing faster than Kudzu vines on a Georgia roadside. This of course creates more than a few practical problems, particularly for bean counters and the definitionally challenged (or is it definitionally dependent?). Although there is no shortage of Internet statistics — computers and computer scientists can't help but capture them — the Internet has become unmeasurable when it comes to totals that matter, such as the number of users it serves or even the number of computers connected to it.

The Internet is also as indescribable as it is unmeasurable. Analogies abound, but all are inapt to a large degree in much the same way that the "horseless carriage" once failed to capture the essence of what would become the automobile. Oxymorons like "information superhighway" are proof that for all the excitement, we have barely entered the horseless carriage phase of the digital revolution. Practically speaking, anyone trying to make sense of the Internet would do well to not take any term too seriously or too far. And anyone who talks of "roadkill" or "off ramps" on the information highway does not know what they are talking about at all.

In the end, the most one can hope for is to gain a sense of the Internet's trajectory by understanding its history and examining a snapshot of the moving target that is its present. This book does an especially good job of both, while also bringing larger issues — such as the proper role of government in the Internet's future — into focus. But in the end, this book will serve you best only if you allow it to convince you to get onto the Internet and explore it for yourself. An hour on the system is worth more than a stack of books or videotapes. Forget the issues, don't fret over the details, and don't worry about making sense of the digital revolution that the Internet portends. Plug your PC into the nearest communications socket, get an account, and just do it.

Paul Saffo
Director of the Institute for the Future

Introduction

Everybody's talking about the Internet. Five years ago, it was mostly computer dweebs like me who were extolling its virtues. Now, it's hard to pick up a magazine or newspaper without hearing about how the Internet is the next big thing.

There are dozens of names for the Internet, but the "Information Superhighway" seems to have become the one. As you read this book, you'll find out why this is both a good description and a lousy one. Because the Internet is changing so fast, any name you give it today will probably seem quaint and out of date a few years from now.

There is one part of the superhighway metaphor that is apropos for the Internet. In my mind, today's Internet is like the U.S. automobile industry in 1895. Roads were being paved, but many were still dirt. What people called highways then would scarcely hold the traffic for a small city now. You had to know a fair amount about mechanics just to own a car. There were many kinds of cars, and people were experimenting with using different kinds of fuel. People who wanted to make money in the automobile industry were making all sorts of investments that we now would laugh heartily at.

The Internet industry is in its early formative stages, just like the automobile industry was 100 years ago. Everyone is acting like they're sure which way the industry will go even though very little is settled about what people will want from the Internet. Most of today's Internet users are doing things that even ten years from now will look silly; on the other hand, a few of today's Internet users will be recognized as visionaries.

This book will show you what's going on today and will give you an idea about what the Internet might look like a few years from now. You may be reading this because you're hot to get on the Internet, or just because you want to know what the fuss is all about. Either way, feel free to make the Internet your destination!

About the NetCruiser Software

You have probably noticed that there is a diskette bound into the back of this book. If you're one of those people who is not yet on the Internet and want to be, the software on that diskette may be exactly what you're looking for.

NetCruiser is software that connects you to the Internet through Netcom, one of the largest Internet service providers in the United States. The NetCruiser software has proven very popular with Internet novices because of its ease of use and installation. Also, Netcom's prices are lower than many other providers if you use the Internet more than once or twice a week.

You don't need to run the software in order to get full benefit from this book. In fact, the software isn't even mentioned again until the very short appendix at the end of the book. There are two reasons for this:

▶ There are many, many different software programs for accessing the Internet. This book talks about many of them but doesn't show preference to any one.

▶ NetCruiser is incredibly easy to set up and start, so almost nothing needs to be said about it.

To run the NetCruiser software, you must have a PC running Microsoft Windows, and you need a 9600-baud (or faster) modem. If you don't have the required setup, or don't want to use Netcom as your service provider, feel free to read the book without using the software. You may want to give it to a friend or use it later. Either way, enjoy the Internet!

What Is the Internet?

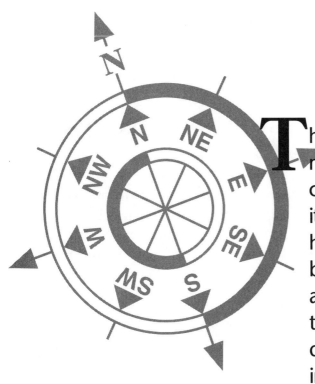

The Internet is many things to many people. To some, it is a computer network; to others, it's millions of people who happen to be linked by this buzzword. You need to know about the different aspects of the Internet before you can decide which part is most important to you.

What Is a Network?

Before you can begin to understand the Internet, you must first know a bit about computer networks in general. This is important because the Internet is a "super network," which can be a bit more confusing to understand than a regular network. A network is a way for two or more computers to communicate electronically.

A computer knows how to compute and how to communicate with you. A computer usually communicates with you by printing information on its screen; you communicate with the computer through the keyboard or by using a mouse. These days, many other kinds of communications between computers and people are

▶ *Communicating between a computer and a person.*

possible, such as through a speaker and microphone, but the screen, keyboard, and mouse are still the most common tools used for communication.

Requirements for a Network

Computers can't communicate with each other in the same way that they communicate with people. Instead, they communicate through a network. Hooking computers up to a network is often tricky because many things must happen first in order for computers on a network to communicate.

Each computer on a network needs to have special internal hardware that can "talk" to the network. This hardware is built into some computers when they are manufactured, but most computers need to have the hardware added.

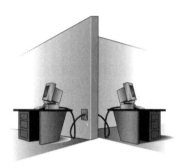

▶ *Communicating between two computers on a network.*

Each computer must also have special software added in or configured for network operation. Very few computers come out of the box ready to be on a network; instead, you have to add software so that the computer knows that it will be communicating with other computers as well as the human at the keyboard. Even the few computers that come with the proper networking software usually need to be tweaked a bit to identify themselves.

The computers must be linked to the network. This is usually done with cable, such as telephone wiring or coaxial cable similar to the cable connected for cable TV. Some networks eliminate cable by having the computers linked by radio signals or light waves. Many computers are networked by connecting them to telephone lines, using the telephone network as part of the computer network.

Deciding to Use a Network

Using a computer on a network can be more complicated than using a computer that is not on a network; there are many reasons why you would want to use a network, however.

▶ In most companies, each employee has information that other employees might want to use. If the computers are linked on a network, it is easier to pass that information around.

▶ If your company has a large database that you want to access, you can connect your computer to the computer with the database, via the network. This is much more efficient than passing the database around to many computers.

▶ E-mail (electronic mail) is one of the most popular, growing forms of communication in many companies. Using e-mail is like sending interoffice memos, but it is much easier to read and process e-mail. For example, most e-mail programs let you automatically sort the mail in your in-box by either the date that the letter was received, or by the person who sent the letter.

▶ There may be hardware attached to one computer that many of the computers on the network want to access. This is common with printers on a network: Instead of buying a printer for each person, a company can purchase fewer printers and put them on the network.

local area network (LAN) A network of computers that are all in the same location, such as an office or building. LANs have become much more common in the past few years as more companies have realized the importance of communication. Some LANs are attached to the Internet, giving each person on the LAN access to Internet resources.

wide area network (WAN) A network of computers spread out over a large distance. Some of the connections in a WAN are typically through telephone lines or over satellites. WANs are also often networks of networks, linking local area networks into a single network.

Of course, not everything about networks is rosy: Networks are prone to problems that often require network specialists to solve. For example, part or all of a network can fail because one of the computers has software that is not working well with the network. Or, there might be a physical problem with part of the network, such as one of the cables being cut. One of the most common network problems is that the network simply has too much traffic with all the computers communicating, and everything becomes too slow to use efficiently.

As you might imagine, this is a gross simplification of how complex networking really is. Fortunately, most networks are advanced enough that the users of the computers on the network don't need to know much about the network in order to share information with other computers.

Understanding Network Basics

The world of networking is full of acronyms, such as LAN, WAN, TCP, IPX, and so on. Networking glossaries have literally hundreds of such TLAs (three-letter acronyms). A few of these acronyms are useful for understanding common computer networks and understanding the Internet in general.

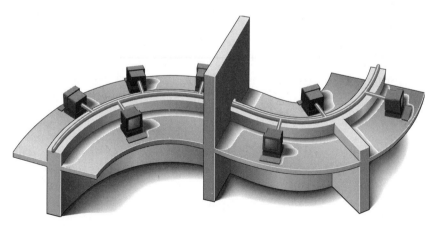

▶ *The "L" in LAN means local, usually just a single building.*

Local Area Networks

The most common networking acronym is *LAN*, which stands for *local area network*. A company in a small office or a single building that has a network probably has a LAN. There are many kinds of LANs, and the type of LAN that a company chooses depends on the kinds of computers the company has, the skills of the LAN support people, the kind of wiring it wants, and so on. Most LANs are based on cable, but others can be connected with radio waves (and are called wireless LANs).

Some companies have more than one LAN in a single building, and sometimes the LANs are interconnected. Interconnecting different kinds of LANs can be very tricky, so many companies standardize on just one type.

Wide Area Networks

When a network grows to include more than a single building or site, it becomes a *WAN*, or *wide area network*. When a LAN becomes a WAN is not precisely defined, but WANs generally rely on the external telephone system or satellite transmission to connect different LANs within a company. Some WANs are truly worldwide.

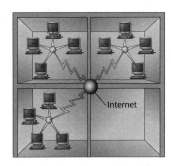

▶ *Wide area networks can be small or very large.*

WANs are important to many companies because they help prevent fragmentation of the different offices. The Bank of America, for example, has its headquarters in San Francisco, branches throughout the state of California, and financial and loan offices in cities throughout the world. The office in Hong Kong would be cut off from day-to-day decisions made at the headquarters without the WAN because communicating by fax and telephone doesn't let people share data easily. By connecting all of its offices on a WAN, a company can also help prevent mistakes in one part of the company from being proliferated in other parts. Of course, the connections between widely spread sites can be hard to manage because there might be thousands of miles of potential problems between two sites.

The Bottom Line on Networks

The alphabet soup of networks can be a bit daunting, although few Internet users know almost anything about the nitty-gritty of networks. The important things to remember are that a network is a collection of connected computers, that a network can be small or huge, and that a network can be in a single room or span the entire globe.

The Internet: A Network of Networks

The Internet is similar to a WAN, but it is structured very differently. A WAN is a single network with a cohesive structure and probably only one group of people responsible for maintaining the whole thing. The Internet consists of thousands of loosely connected networks and no single group is responsible for it. Believe it or not, this is the beauty of the Internet.

The one unifying theme for how the Internet is put together is that each network on the Internet is independent, but each network communicates with the Internet using the same networking language. Thus, your company may have a LAN, and the network administrator might allow access from the LAN to the Internet. Your LAN is still your LAN, but it is also part of the Internet. Your company is responsible for its part of the LAN and somewhat responsible for its connection to the Internet, but is not responsible for anything else that goes on. On the Internet itself, the structure of the connected networks doesn't really matter.

Internet Analogies

The Internet is like a library. In a library, each publication has its own structure and its own organization, unrelated to other publications. The publications are organized on the shelves using a system (card catalog numbers) that is quite different from the system used internally (the table of contents, the index, and so on). If you are reading one book and it refers to a another book, you can use the library's main catalog to see if that other book exists in the library and if so, where it's shelved.

By the way, there are hundreds of different analogies for the Internet. The information superhighway is just one of them.

The way that each network connects to the Internet is through hardware called a *router*. Routers do many things, but their main purpose with regard to the Internet is to keep the information on the Internet flowing to its correct location. When some data comes to a router, it checks whether that information is supposed to go through that router. If the information does go through, the router tries to send it on the best possible route.

Another Internet analogy is to think of the Internet as the postal service, with routers serving as local post offices (see, there really are lots of Internet analogies). When a post office receives a letter, it first checks to see if the address is local to that post office. If not, the post office passes the letter along after determining the best way to get the letter to a post office close to the destination address. If the post office is a tiny one, the letter may first be sent to a nearby large post office, which then routes the letter to a large post office closest to the desired location, and so on.

router A device that connects two networks, allowing only certain traffic to pass through. Routers are used at almost every intersection on the Internet to both limit traffic going to smaller networks and to help choose the most efficient way to get packets to their desired destinations. Some routers cost under $2,000, although others cost well over $25,000.

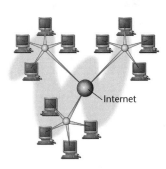

▶ *The Internet connects thousands of LANs and WANs.*

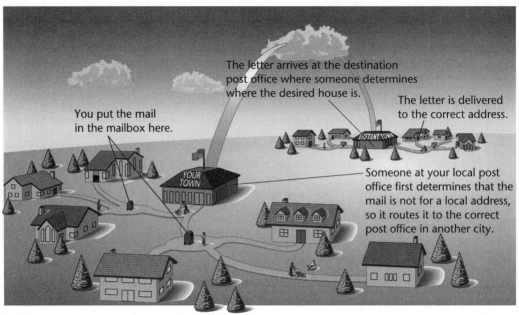

The letter arrives at the destination post office where someone determines where the desired house is.

You put the mail in the mailbox here.

The letter is delivered to the correct address.

Someone at your local post office first determines that the mail is not for a local address, so it routes it to the correct post office in another city.

▶ *By one analogy, the Internet is similar to the postal service.*

Using this analogy, your house is like the networks on the Internet: The post office has no idea how you route letters within your house after the mail carrier drops a letter into the family mailbox. For example, the first person to get home may pull out his or her mail and put the rest of the mail in a pile on the kitchen table. On the other hand, the first person to get mail from the mailbox may separate the mail by recipient or choose to leave the mail in the mailbox for the next person to deal with. After the mail gets beyond the router (the post office), it is up to the local network (your household) to deal with it however it sees fit.

History of the Internet

The Internet is still in its formative stages. The look and feel of the Internet today is very different from what it was just five years ago, and the Internet will probably look very different again five years from now. Thus, it is quite useful to look at the Internet's history so that you can see how the Internet got to be the way that it is.

When the Internet was first being designed in 1969, computer networks were much more primitive than they are today. Early networks were fragile, and the smallest problem on one of the computers on the network could cause the whole network to crash. On many early networks, simply turning off one of the computers on the network caused the network to stop working.

ARPAnet

The U.S. Defense Department realized that computer networks were very important, but it was hesitant to rely on such fragile systems. Therefore, it started researching how to create networks that were more robust and could survive during wartime. The concepts that were developed through the life of the project have now become almost second nature for most computer networks. The network was originally called *ARPAnet*, after *Advanced Research Projects Agency*, the agency that was its parent.

ARPAnet The network run by the U.S. Defense Department's Advanced Research Projects Agency that was the original backbone of the Internet. The ARPAnet was originally intended as a research network that would also link Defense Department affiliates. ARPA handed the ARPAnet to the U.S. National Science Foundation, which turned it into the NSFnet.

The Defense Department had to deal with another major problem related to reliability. Computers made by different companies could not exist on the same network because their manufacturers supported only their own networking systems. To provide flexibility during wartime, it was important that the Defense Department be able to interchange computers on a network if necessary.

Although ARPAnet was being built with military funds, it was largely developed at universities. A few parts were classified, but most of the ARPAnet was quite open. The idea behind this openness was to get the most input possible for making the network more stable, more robust, more available, and more useful. The project was a great success.

List of Commercial Services on the Web (and Net)

Last updated 14 September 1994 - **What's New in Commercial Sites**

Please send email to *hhh@mit.edu* to add entries to these lists. A short description will be placed here, while a full description will be placed in the **What's New in Commercial Sites list**.

Also see the lists for:

- What's New in Commercial Sites
- Commercial Web Servers - companies that will create/host your pages

Businesses and Companies

Select a letter to move to that section in the directory:

A B C D E F G H I J K L M N O P Q R S T U V W X Y Z Commercial Servers

    A

1. A+ Marketing (8/28/94)
2. A Aa Building Inspection Services (8/28/94)
3. AAA Advertising (9/4/94)
4. Absolutely Fresh Flowers (7/20/94)
5. Academia Latinoamericana de Español (6/13/94)
6. Access Market Square, located in Salt Lake City, Utah (7/8/94)
7. adfx - Virtual Advertising, HTML preparation and placement (6/6/94)
8. Adobe ftp server

▶ *In the past couple of years, thousands of companies have started using the Internet for communication with customers and potential customers. This is just a small part of a long list of such companies.*

The many open discussions on the ARPAnet about how to optimize the technology led to other discussions, such as finding the best possible way to pass information around this new network. Electronic mail was one of the first things to be standardized, followed by file transfer, and then news. None of these features were developed commercially or privately: It was all done by people who were excited about creating an open standard that could be used by anyone. This educational orientation is what gave the Internet the flavor it has today.

The Internet in the '90s

In the past five years, the Internet has changed a great deal. In the late 1980s, most of the people on the Internet were university people, ex-university people who had kept their accounts active, some computer corporations, and a few others. In the past few years, however, many people outside these groups have gotten on the Internet.

Commercialization of the Internet

The biggest change has been the commercialization of the Internet. This term, used widely in newspaper and TV news stories about the Internet, doesn't really mean much because commercial content has been on the Internet for more than a decade. The big difference is that now more people can buy Internet accounts (instead of having to get one through a university, government agency, and so on) and companies can easily set up shop on the Internet so that Internet users can find them.

The Foundation Remains

Even with all these changes, many parts of the Internet look much like they did ten years ago. ARPAnet created a technical foundation that is alive, well, and growing old quite gracefully. The social foundation laid by thousands of university people and other ARPAnet/Internet users over the last decade is also surprisingly intact as well, although showing a bit more strain as more people who are unaware of the Internet's colorful history go online.

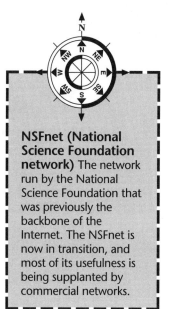

NSFnet (National Science Foundation network) The network run by the National Science Foundation that was previously the backbone of the Internet. The NSFnet is now in transition, and most of its usefulness is being supplanted by commercial networks.

Where Is the Internet?

You have probably heard people say that they are "on the Internet." Now that you know a bit more about the nature of the Internet, you can see how that sounds a bit misleading. No one is really on the Internet: How many people do you know who are on a network connected to another network? When people say they are "on the Internet," they mean they can connect to the Internet.

Finding the Internet

There is no way to define where the Internet is. The hardware for the Internet consists of the computers on the network and the cables between them. Therefore, in one sense, the Internet is at every computer on the network and on all the telephone cables, as well as all the satellite parts of the phone network.

The most interesting part of the Internet, though, is the people who use it, not the hardware. Most people on the Internet today are connected to it through personal computers or terminals in their homes or offices. When you use your personal computer to connect to a larger computer on the Internet, you and your computer become part of the Internet. Even when you aren't in front of your computer, people can reach you by sending electronic mail that will be waiting for you when you next connect to the Internet.

If you count people as the most important resource on the Internet, then it's easy to say where the Internet is: all over the world! You can find people with Internet connections in almost every country in the world. Of course, some countries — such as the United States — have more connections than other countries, but people everywhere are on the Internet.

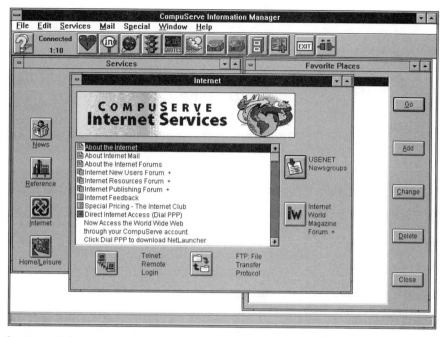

▶ One of the more popular ways to reach the Internet is through CompuServe, whose Internet section is shown here.

Who Owns the Internet?

Because the Internet is a network of networks, no one owns the whole thing. Each company, university, government, and organization owns its own part of the network. Different companies and government agencies own the "glue" (hardware and software) that holds the various parts of the Internet together, but that does not mean that they own the information passing through the Internet.

ARPA and NSF

As discussed earlier, the Advanced Research Projects Agency (ARPA) of the U.S. Department of Defense owned and operated the backbone of Internet in the United States, and then transferred that authority to the National Science Foundation (NSF), which still

CIX (Commercial Internet Exchange) The first major industry group for companies that provide Internet access. Because the CIX consists of competitors in a constantly changing market, CIX is a somewhat volatile group. CIX also lobbies the U.S. government on Internet-related issues.

▶ *There are many commercial Internet vendors that link cities throughout the United States. Some are large and link hundreds of cities, while others are small and may link just two cities.*

maintains some of the backbone (the NSF part of the Internet is called NSFnet). However, in recent years, the backbone has been augmented by many companies and by other government agencies, and the NSF has sold many parts of what was the NSFnet to commercial Internet vendors. Connections to the rest of the world are owned and operated by both governmental and private companies as well.

CIX

Today, more and more network traffic in the United States uses parts of the Internet not on the NSFnet. Some commercial companies banded together to form the CIX (Commercial Internet Exchange) so that they can link their services together in a somewhat cohesive fashion. Other companies run their own parts of the Internet and have made individual arrangements for traffic to enter and leave their networks at various points. In the future, hundreds of companies and organizations may make up the backbone.

Maintaining the Internet

You may think that this situation could be a nightmare for maintenance and support, and it often is! Fortunately, when a small part of the network fails, the owner of that part fixes the problem while traffic goes around it. However, if one of the larger Internet backbones has problems, those problems are felt throughout the entire Internet.

No one company owns or maintains the content of the Internet, such as files that users download or postings in Usenet news. Anyone can make any kind of information available, even things that you might not want to be exposed to. There is no one place to complain about something on the Internet, as each site on the Internet is responsible for its own content.

Who Runs the Internet?

Just because no one owns the Internet, don't assume no one helps keep it running smoothly. Since the beginning, the Internet has been developed and nurtured by thousands of volunteers who wanted to see it thrive. The situation is the same today.

The Internet Society

The main group that oversees the development of the Internet is the Internet Society, commonly called ISOC. ISOC is pretty much a coordinating agency for other groups rather than primarily a membership group; ISOC has no official governmental power although it has become the center of focus for people who want to participate in the care and management of the Internet.

ISOC oversees many voluntary groups, including

▶ Internet Architecture Board (IAB)

▶ Internet Engineering Task Force (IETF)

▶ Internet Assigned Number Authority (IANA)

▶ Internet Engineering Steering Group (IESG)

▶ Internet Research Task Force (IRTF)

RFCs (Requests for Comments) Documents that define the technical aspects of the Internet. Originally, these documents were used to get input from other technical users of the Internet before standards were set down, and many RFCs today still serve that purpose. Other RFCs are simply statements of reality.

Internet Architecture Board (IAB) The group that oversees Internet technical issues. It oversees the IETF and the IRTF, and acts as a liaison with other nontechnical Internet bodies.

Internet Society (ISOC) A voluntary group that acts as a focal point for Internet building. The ISOC has been particularly active in bringing non-U.S. users onto the Internet and in coordinating other Internet-related groups.

▶ K-12 Committee

▶ Disaster Assistance Committee

▶ Internet Operations Forum

An advisory council consisting of many ISOC-related organizations helps ISOC with its coordination and planning.

Each year, ISOC hosts a large conference — INET — where the state of the Internet is discussed. Because ISOC is an international organization, this conference is often held outside the United States. People from all over the world come to talk about how the Internet will look in the future, how countries such as the U.S. can help much smaller countries get fully connected to the Internet, how commercialization will change the Internet, and so on. There are also many technical discussions about Internet protocols and the like.

ISOC's Internet Society News

The *Internet Society News*, ISOC's quarterly publication, is probably the best printed source of information about the Internet. (Of course, the very best information is found online.) The *Internet Society News* has many columns, including fascinating stories about the introduction of the Internet to small countries, legal aspects of Internet communication, new Internet services, book reviews, and so on. There is also a list of all the new online Internet standards documents, as well as contact information for the most important, and well-known, people on the Internet.

For more information about ISOC:

Internet Society
12020 Sunrise Valley Drive, Suite 270
Reston, VA 22091
703-648-9888
membership@isoc.org

The Internet Engineering Task Force

The Internet Engineering Task Force (IETF) is one of the most important organizations supporting the Internet because it sets the technical guidelines for how the network operates. All networking is difficult, and you can imagine how hard it is to get millions of different computers that use different operating systems to talk to each other. The IETF is a superb example of how technical prowess helps overcome potential disasters. The following description of the IETF comes from a document called "The Tao of the IETF," also known as "RFC 1539:"

Internet Engineering Task Force (IETF) The group that oversees the technical standards on which the Internet is based. The IETF is an all-volunteer organization and is heaven for computer geeks. The technical decisions made by the IETF affect how the Internet functions, how fast it operates, and how well it will last in the future.

Internet Research Task Force (IRTF) The research arm of the IAB. The IRTF looks at issues that affect the Internet in the future, such as what happens after lots of growth, and how certain technologies will affect Internet traffic.

The IETF is a loosely self-organized group of people who make technical and other contributions to the engineering and evolution of the Internet and its technologies. It is the principal body engaged in the development of new Internet standard specifications. The IETF mission includes:

▶ Identifying and proposing solutions for pressing operational and technical problems in the Internet.

▶ Specifying the development or usage of protocols and the near-term architecture to solve such technical problems for the Internet.

▶ Making recommendations to the Internet Engineering Steering Group (IESG) regarding the standardization of protocols and protocol usage in the Internet.

▶ Facilitating the transfer of technology from the Internet Research Task Force (IRTF) to the wider Internet community.

▶ Providing a forum for the exchange of information within the Internet community among vendors, users, researchers, agency contractors, and network managers.

The IETF Plenary meeting is not a conference, though technical presentations are given. The IETF is not a traditional standards organization, but it produces many standards. The IETF consists of volunteers who meet three times a year to fulfill the IETF mission. There is no membership in the IETF. Anyone may register for and attend any meeting. The closest thing there is to being an IETF member is being on the IETF or Working Group mailing lists. These mailing lists provide the best information about current IETF activities and their focus.

How Many People Are on the Internet?

Counting people on the Internet is not much different from counting jelly beans in a jar at the county fair: If you make one incorrect assumption, your guess is going to be way, way off. With the Internet, you can make many incorrect assumptions, which is probably why you have heard so many different numbers about the population of the Internet.

Counting Problems

It is not really surprising that it's difficult to count the number of people on the Internet. Users don't have to register in a central location before getting on the Internet. In fact, Internet providers don't register in one central location either because they may be part of someone else's network, and therefore don't even have to register their network. This means that counting the number of Internet users is probably impossible.

Deciding Who to Count

The problem is further compounded by the question of what "on the Internet" means. There are many different levels of services on the Internet, and you may not consider people with only minimal access as really being "on the Internet." Millions of people can send electronic mail through the Internet but can't take advantage of any of the other useful features covered in this book. A subset of those millions can send mail and read Usenet news, but nothing else. A smaller subset can send mail, read Usenet news, and use the many interesting services such as the World Wide Web and Gopher. It's impossible to measure any of these groups.

Because there is no central place for all Internet users to register, how do the experts come up with numbers like "3 million" and "20 million"? Well, they're not just guessing; they're trying to extrapolate what data they do have into useful numbers, but there is much dissension about the methodology.

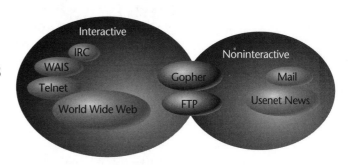

▶ *Before you can even start to count who is on the Internet, you have to define what it takes to be in one group or the other.*

mail Messages sent over the Internet use the Simple Mail Transport Protocol (SMTP). Internet mail is by far the most popular and most used feature of the Internet. Most of the estimated 20 million Internet users — if there are even that many — have only mail access.

Counting Host Computers

The only numbers that people are sure of is the number of host computers on the Internet, which is about 3 million. However, it is not at all clear how to convert that number into number of people. Many of those hosts have no real users; some have thousands. Some sites, such as universities, have a single computer for all incoming electronic mail, but most of the users also have accounts on other computers at the site. If this situation isn't taken into account, everybody using the Internet could be counted twice (or more).

The method of multiplying the number of hosts by a constant is really quite silly. Such a method is analagous to determining the population of a city by counting the number of buildings in the city and multiplying that number by how many people could be in the buildings. You can ask a building's owner, "How many people use your building?" — but the answer would be meaningless. Most buildings are not used to capacity. Further, many people "belong" to more than one building (their home, their office, the restaurants they frequent, and so on), which can lead to a huge overcount. Also, people come in from outside the city to use some of the buildings, which could lead to a potential undercount. On the Internet, the method is even worse because, quite often, no one will answer questions about host computers and their usage.

Changing the Focus

Maybe it's time to get over the idea of having to count how many people are on the Internet and just start enjoying the ones who are. Clearly, millions of people around the world have at least mail access to the Internet, and millions more have additional access as well. If only 10 percent decided to publish interesting writings or pictures, or to contribute to ongoing discussions, imagine how incredible the Internet would be!

Popular Networks that Are Not the Internet

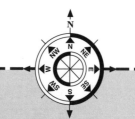

The Internet is not the only online service that you can use for sending e-mail, keeping up with the latest news, downloading interesting files, and chatting. Many people were doing these kinds of things before the Internet was widely available. One of the best known online services, *CompuServe*, had many of these features in 1979, long before almost anyone could get accounts on the Internet.

Major Online Services

Some of the larger services are partially connected to the Internet. Almost every major online service lets you send mail back and forth with Internet users, although some put restrictions on this feature. No major service gives full Internet connectivity like many of the smaller Internet providers you can probably find in your area.

On the other hand, large online services have many excellent features that you cannot find on the Internet. Hundreds of computer companies have technical support areas on the major services, and questions asked in these areas are often definitively answered within hours. Many topics are discussed much more actively on the major services than on the Internet. Some services also provide much better, friendlier interfaces than even the most modern Internet programs.

America Online A large bulletin board system with over 1 million users. America Online, also called AOL, was the first of the "big three" bulletin board systems (Prodigy, America Online, CompuServe) to have more than just a mail connection to the Internet. It introduced both a Gopher client and a Usenet news client in spring of 1994.

CompuServe Probably the best-known bulletin board system with over 2 million users. CompuServe was one of the earliest of the large systems not directly connected to the Internet to offer Internet mail access to its users. Recently, CompuServe has embraced the Internet by giving its users access to features such as Usenet news.

bulletin board systems (BBSs)
Computers that allow people to dial through modems and use their services. Some BBSs are on the Internet, although most are not. BBSs often have downloadable files, discussion areas, and other features that make them popular. You can use some BBSs for free, while others charge a monthly or hourly fee.

Bulletin Board Services

In the case of online services, bigger doesn't necessarily mean better. Smaller online services, called *BBSs* (bulletin board systems), offer more Internet connectivity than the larger services. They also have their own features, such as discussion areas, games, and files, that are not found on the Internet. Unfortunately, many small BBSs don't have any connection to the Internet — not even mail exchange.

Making Your Choice

When you see an online service company, large or small, advertising that you can use its service to get on the Internet, be careful to find out how much of the Internet it offers. The largest services offer you some of the Internet, but none of them offer full connections. In many communities, you have a few different BBSs and Internet providers to choose from, and there is probably a range of how well these services let you use the Internet.

▶ *America Online's opening screen.*

▶ *CompuServe's opening screen.*

Is the Internet the Information Superhighway?

By now, you may be getting weary of all the highway metaphors for the Internet. Gone are the days when people got excited about a new highway being built near their homes. But the Internet is exciting, and it is a bit sad that it has been saddled with this metaphor (and all the silly jokes that go with it).

Seeing the Future

Part of the problem with this metaphor is that it's not at all clear whether there will be one grand integration of information, phone service, and cable television. Sure, it can be done, but the costs are still unknown. Worse yet, there doesn't seem to be much demand for all of these services to come into your home or office on a single

▶ *Many people have called the Internet the information superhighway, but this may not be the most appropriate analogy given the many kinds of things the Internet does besides give you information.*

cable. Five years from now, we may laugh at the idea that the superhighway was imminent and find that the Internet is nothing more than an interesting, busy city street.

Maybe the most unfortunate characteristic of the highway analogy is that most of us think of highways as places for cars; no one gets out of their cars on the highway to talk or ask each other questions and so on. Sure, the highways lead to towns where that happens, but the analogy indicates that you end up in a different town, not your home.

Finding Other Analogies

Using the tools of the Internet, however, you can meet people and share information from your home. The highway does not matter: It's the people you can meet and the information you can find. And you can do it from the comfort of your own home (or your office, if that's where you use your computer). Maybe it's time we find other analogies that emphasize the people and information on the Internet instead of the computers and network itself.

The Internet is like, well, the Internet. But it is also like:

▶ *In the library of the future, people will look up things other than just reference materials. For example, they may use the library to talk to other researchers or to look up historical video documents.*

▶ A library where the books can be interactive, the catalog is vast, some of the books are for sale, and there are many rooms where talking is not only allowed, but encouraged. If you want to hang out in the reference area the whole time, fine, but many people drift from the talking rooms into the music section into the magazine racks, and back again.

▶ A university with many libraries, coffee houses, stores, seminar rooms, and museums. Not that all of us want to relive our undergraduate days, but there were probably parts we all liked, such as sitting around chatting about bicycles, sharing notes about the hard parts of a technical class, scanning the bulletin boards for free or cheap entertainment, searching for the best conversations at a large party, and discovering really weird old books in the library.

Is the Internet Ready for Business?

The Internet has many uses and a great deal of potential for the future. We still don't know to what extent American businesses will embrace the Internet as a medium for advertising, education, and commerce. So far, only a tiny number of companies do significant business on the Internet, but the number is certainly growing.

Advertising on the Internet

There's no doubt that the Internet will become a popular place for advertising and promotion. The World Wide Web is designed for the kinds of multimedia that can make the Internet more attractive than most other online services. Already, you can see previews from popular movies, hear hit music, and look through interactive demonstrations of automobiles. The kinds of advertising on the Internet will expand even more as creative marketers team up with software and design experts to share their skills.

Financial Transactions

One big question is how safe the Internet will be for financial transactions. There is very little security between computers on the

▶ First Virtual was one of the first companies to make paying for services on the Internet without using your credit card easy. You set up an account with First Virtual, and companies that also have accounts with it can then accept payments from you without your revealing your credit card number.

Internet, and eavesdroppers can listen in on electronic conversations between computers all too easily. Those conversations might include your credit card number, the identification number for your ATM card, or other personal information.

This is not to say that it is impossible to conduct financial transactions on the Internet. If the messages sent between the two computers are encoded in a way that an eavesdropper cannot understand, it doesn't really matter whether or not anyone is listening. However, both computers must agree on the encoding method before the transaction happens. Furthermore, they must use a system that cannot be broken by eavesdroppers with sophisticated software.

Security Methods

Fortunately, there are methods being tested and deployed today that make these kinds of financial transactions possible. Because of the great potential for people ordering online, many banks and other financial institutions are researching security techniques and will soon be selecting the ones they feel are the safest and easiest to use. Unfortunately, there may be more than one standard, meaning that Internet users may have to keep track of different ordering and payment methods for different stores.

You may have heard people say, "Never send your credit card number over the Internet." This advice may be correct in theory (someone might be snooping on the connection between you and the site to which you are sending your credit card number), but it is probably more strident than it needs to be. After all, most people trust their credit card numbers and their signatures every day to strangers in gas stations, restaurants, convenience stores, and so on. It is unclear whether financial transactions conducted over the Internet, even those that aren't encoded, will be any more prone to theft than today's standard financial transactions.

PART 2

Internet Basics

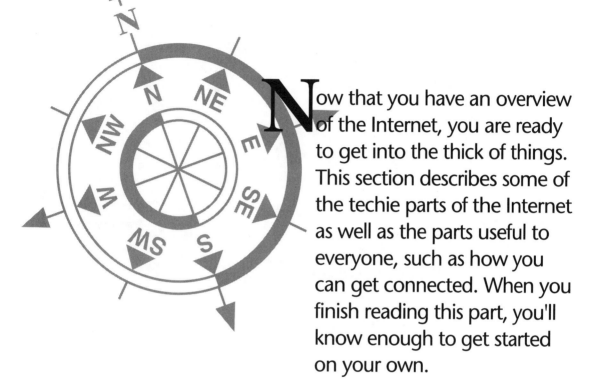

Now that you have an overview of the Internet, you are ready to get into the thick of things. This section describes some of the techie parts of the Internet as well as the parts useful to everyone, such as how you can get connected. When you finish reading this part, you'll know enough to get started on your own.

The Hardware of Internet Connections

Most people initially think of hardware when they think about computer networks. On the Internet, however, the software is more interesting than the hardware. Of course, the most interesting part is the people and what they do with all the hardware and software. But, because most people usually have an easier time visualizing hardware than they do visualizing software, I'll discuss hardware first.

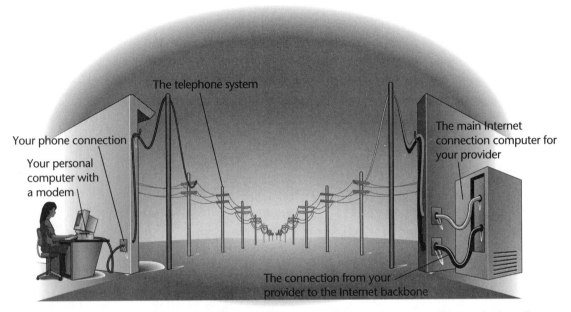

The telephone system

Your phone connection

Your personal
computer with
a modem

The main Internet
connection computer for
your provider

The connection from your
provider to the Internet backbone

▶ *The Internet is much more than just the larger computers on the network. It includes all the computers and connections of each person on the Internet.*

Because the Internet is a network of networks, and each network consists of computers and the connections between them, Internet hardware looks like other computer network hardware, just much larger. You cannot tell the difference between the Internet and most WANs just by looking at the hardware.

Basic Components

As discussed earlier, when you log on to one of these networks, you and your personal computer then become part of the Internet. Thus, the hardware of the Internet includes all the home and business PCs that are used by Internet users. The phone lines you use are also part of the Internet because you use them to hook up to your Internet access provider.

Computers

The computers that are directly on the Internet are often larger and more powerful than standard PCs, but not always. In fact, almost any kind of computer, from the largest mainframe to the standard desktop PC, can run the software needed to connect directly to the Internet.

Data Lines

Some computers on the Internet are connected through standard phone lines, but many are connected with dedicated data lines — lines that are used only for networking. Dedicated data lines usually are more reliable than standard phone lines and often transmit data faster.

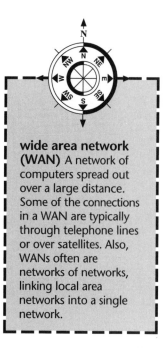

wide area network (WAN) A network of computers spread out over a large distance. Some of the connections in a WAN are typically through telephone lines or over satellites. Also, WANs often are networks of networks, linking local area networks into a single network.

Today, most dedicated data lines are made of the same substance as phone lines: copper wire. However, dedicated data lines go through different switches than basic phone lines, because the way to make a connection between each end is different. Other dedicated lines use fiber-optic cable, which can carry much more data than standard copper wire.

TCP/IP

The computers on the Internet run many different operating systems, but they all have one thing in common: They communicate with each other by using a common networking language called *TCP/IP* (Transmission Control Protocol over Internet Protocol). TCP/IP is the common protocol among all Internet computers. In a sense, it is the software that makes the Internet network hang together.

TCP The standard used on the Internet to identify the kind of information in packets. TCP, which stands for Transmission Control Protocol, is almost always used with the IP standard, and you normally hear of them together as TCP/IP. TCP also makes sure that data is passed with no errors.

You don't need to know about TCP/IP to be able to use the Internet, but if you have any technical curiosity, TCP/IP is worth investigating a little bit. On the other hand, if you're not interested in terms like "bytes" and "address," feel free to skip the next few pages.

Origin of TCP/IP

TCP/IP initially became a standard on the Internet because it was easy to implement and the specification for it was available to everyone. Another feature that made it popular was that the standard is independent of hardware, meaning you can get TCP/IP to work on any kind of networking hardware and cabling.

TCP/IP encompasses two standards: TCP and IP. On the Internet, nearly everyone uses the two standards together; that's why they are almost always discussed together.

Basic TCP/IP Roles

TCP and IP play different roles in getting two computers to talk. IP is the low-level method for moving information from one computer to another, and TCP is the high-level method for expressing what the information is and ensuring that the information is understandable.

If you think of the Internet as a book, IP is pages and TCP is the language in which the book is written. The book might be about anything at all: The pages and the language are quite different than the content. However, without pages, there would be nothing to write on, and without a language, the reader would have no idea what he or she was looking at.

TCP Functions

The important parts of TCP are

▶ Assuring that the information passes through the Internet with no data loss.

▶ Assuring that the information is not accidentally or maliciously modified while it is traveling through the network.

▶ Retransmitting information that does not arrive correctly.

▶ Enabling two computers to set up an extended conversation while millions of other conversations are going on.

▶ Providing methods for splitting a long message into different sections and having those sections reassembled in the right order at the destination.

IP The standard used by computers to transmit information over the Internet. IP stands for Internet Protocol and defines how the information will look as it travels between computers, not what the computers will do with it. IP also defines how Internet addresses work.

IP Functions

The important parts of IP include

▶ A basic definition of how data flows over Internet hardware.

▶ Methods for identifying each computer on the Internet so that users can identify where information came from and indicate where it's going.

▶ A system that allows information to be split into smaller parts as it moves through some parts of the Internet.

▶ A set of different higher-level protocols (TCP is the only one of interest here, however).

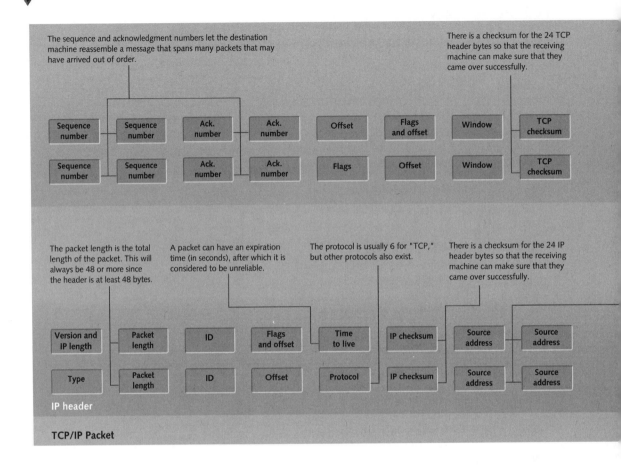

The sequence and acknowledgment numbers let the destination machine reassemble a message that spans many packets that may have arrived out of order.

There is a checksum for the 24 TCP header bytes so that the receiving machine can make sure that they came over successfully.

| Sequence number | Sequence number | Ack. number | Ack. number | Offset | Flags and offset | Window | TCP checksum |
| Sequence number | Sequence number | Ack. number | Ack. number | Flags | Offset | Window | TCP checksum |

The packet length is the total length of the packet. This will always be 48 or more since the header is at least 48 bytes.

A packet can have an expiration time (in seconds), after which it is considered to be unreliable.

The protocol is usually 6 for "TCP," but other protocols also exist.

There is a checksum for the 24 IP header bytes so that the receiving machine can make sure that they came over successfully.

| Version and IP length | Packet length | ID | Flags and offset | Time to live | IP checksum | Source address | Source address |
| Type | Packet length | ID | Offset | Protocol | IP checksum | Source address | Source address |

IP header

TCP/IP Packet

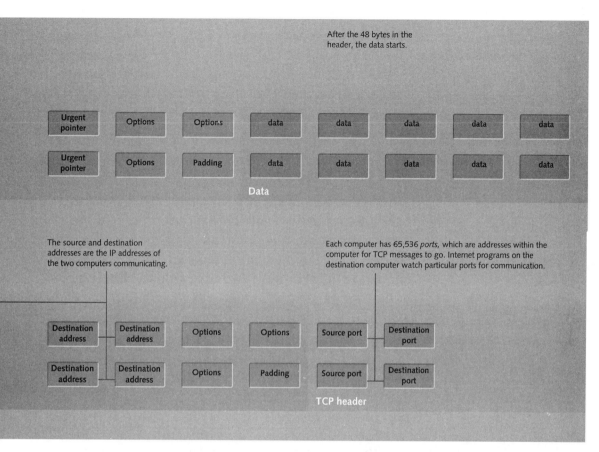

After the 48 bytes in the header, the data starts.

| Urgent pointer | Options | Options | data | data | data | data | data |

| Urgent pointer | Options | Padding | data | data | data | data | data |

Data

The source and destination addresses are the IP addresses of the two computers communicating.

Each computer has 65,536 *ports*, which are addresses within the computer for TCP messages to go. Internet programs on the destination computer watch particular ports for communication.

| Destination address | Destination address | Options | Options | Source port | Destination port |

| Destination address | Destination address | Options | Padding | Source port | Destination port |

TCP header

▶ *The structure of a TCP/IP packet. Each block is a byte. Some of the interesting parts of the headers are also explained here. If you understand all this, you could have a promising future in Internet system administration.*

port A number that helps TCP identify what kind of service you are asking for from another computer. Most common Internet features such as Gopher have standard port numbers (for example, 70 for Gopher) that client software uses if you do not specify a different port number. The only time you need to know about ports is when a server requires that you use a nonstandard port number to communicate.

What Does TCP/IP Do?

What does all this mean? Basically, when two computers converse over the Internet, TCP/IP can guarantee that the conversation is complete, accurate, and unaffected by problems in Internet hardware.

If you can believe that TCP/IP lets the computers on the Internet communicate safely and easily, the next most interesting thing about this protocol is how each computer on the Internet has its own unique address. Maybe this doesn't sound so amazing to you: After all, every house with a telephone has its own unique telephone number made up of ten digits. However, addressing on computer networks is anything but easy.

How Does TCP/IP Do It?

Every computer on a TCP/IP network has an address made up of four numbers. (Actually, addressing is part of IP, so the same is true of any IP network, not just TCP/IP networks.) Each number is one byte long, meaning that the number is between 0 and 255. The address is usually shown with periods between the numbers. Thus, an address might be "172.201.25.1" or "192.47.9.220," for example.

If you're good at math, you may have already figured out that more than 4 billion addresses are possible using this scheme. Unfortunately, that isn't exactly true, because of the way the addresses are assigned to people on the Internet. If you have a TCP/IP network that isn't connected to the Internet, you can use whatever addresses you want. However, if you want to connect your network to the Internet, you must ask for a set of addresses for your network and then promise to use only those addresses.

To make routers work better and faster, each computer on a network on the Internet usually has the same first three numbers as the other computers on that network (and each network usually has fewer than 250 computers on it). When you ask for a set of addresses, you usually get a block of 256, even though your network may have only a few computers on it. Because of this, the Internet is running out of addresses, but the network gurus are busy coming up with better addressing schemes that will change the way IP works, probably within the next few years.

Understanding the Domain Name System

As you have already seen, you specify Internet hosts as names, such as "jsc.nasa.gov" or "proper.com." Although it is not really part of the TCP/IP protocols, there is a universal mechanism for converting these names to the IP address that TCP/IP understands. This mechanism, called the *domain name system,* or DNS, is used on every Internet computer so that you almost never need to know the IP address of a computer you are trying to reach.

Basically, when computer A wants to convert the name of computer B to the IP address of computer B, it makes a DNS request to a local master DNS server. The master DNS servers have only one level of domain listed in their conversion tables. (If they had all of them, the databases would have millions of entries.) But the master DNS servers do know how to hand off the request to other servers that know the specifics for domains with more than one level in them. The request may be bounced to one or two more DNS servers, but you will get a result eventually.

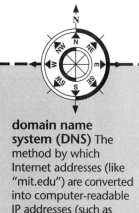

domain name system (DNS) The method by which Internet addresses (like "mit.edu") are converted into computer-readable IP addresses (such as "182.156.12.24"). The DNS is one of the most flexible and powerful technical features of the Internet, allowing computers to appear and disappear from the Internet without causing problems. It also makes sending messages much easier because there does not have to be a central repository of all names.

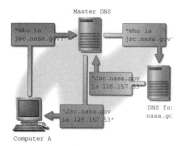

▶ *Finding the address of a computer by its name is a multistep process that often involves many computers.*

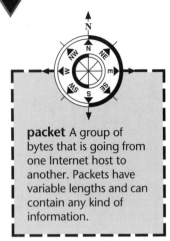

packet A group of bytes that is going from one Internet host to another. Packets have variable lengths and can contain any kind of information.

For example, if computer A wants to know the IP address of "jsc.nasa.gov," it makes a request to a master DNS server. That server doesn't know the IP address of "jsc.nasa.gov," but it knows another DNS server (probably at NASA) that knows all the addresses for anything that ends with "nasa.gov." The master DNS server sends out the request to that server, which replies to computer A with the full IP address.

Data Packets

When two computers communicate by using TCP/IP, they send data *packets*. A packet is simply a group of bytes that are arranged in a well-defined order. The beginning of each packet has particular information about the data in the packet, such as where the data is supposed to go and some information about the format of the data. Following this header, the rest of the packet is the data (the real information) that is being sent. The packet can be up to 65,536 bytes long.

The packet's header has two parts: the IP part followed by the TCP part. Each part is 24 bytes long. Within each part is some arcane information, but you can probably understand some of the important parts as well. Of course, none of this is important to 99 percent of Internet users, but every crowd has a technogeek who wants to know exactly how the inside of everything looks.

Connected versus Unconnected Computers

Millions of computers are on the Internet. You may wonder whether all of them are connected all the time. If you've ever had a computer lock up on you (we all have), you know that there are many times when a computer is just not running. The same is true for computers on the Internet.

Part-time Connections

You may remember from the discussion about the history of the Internet that one of the primary design goals was to make the network work just fine even if one or more of the computers on it went down. That part of the Internet works just great. It works so well that, in order to save money, many companies have computers that are connected to the Internet for only a couple of hours a day. Usually, these are computers that use modems to dial into an Internet network. To save phone bill costs, the computers dial in only when necessary.

Because the Internet is a network of networks, as long as the network to which you attach your computer is working, you don't need to worry about having your computer working all the time. Mechanisms are built into the Internet software for handling situations such as someone trying to access a computer that isn't connected

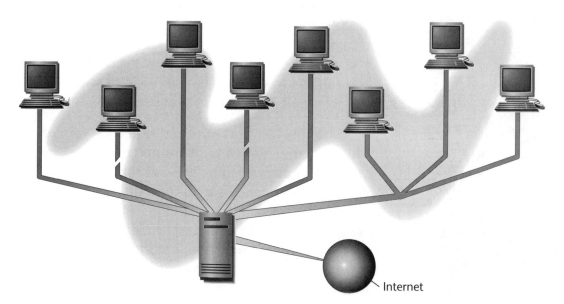

Internet

▶ *Many companies like to keep their computers on the Internet all the time, while others choose to have their computers on only part of the time.*

UUCP A common method of communication for computers that are connected to the Internet only part of the time. UUCP, which stands for UNIX-to-UNIX-Copy, is a very old standard that allows mail messages, Usenet news, and files to be transferred from computer to computer. It has become less popular in recent years, although many bulletin board systems still use it to pass mail.

e-mail Electronic mail; Internet users often use the term e-mail to differentiate their electronic mail messages from mail delivered by the U.S. Postal Service, which the rest of the world is more familiar with.

to the Internet at the moment. The software is even designed to make it easy for you to move your computer from one part of the Internet to another without anyone having to know that you moved the computer.

People are connected to the Internet also, though no one is connected all the time. Let's face it: Life exists beyond the Internet! But many mechanisms built into the Internet make it easy for people to connect for only a few minutes a day yet still seem as though they have a big presence there.

Electronic Mail

As you will see later, the most common way for two people to communicate over the Internet is by using electronic mail, commonly called *e-mail*. In one sense, e-mail is like regular mail: It is delivered to your mailbox and waits for you to look through it. When you are not connected to the Internet, your e-mail just accumulates in your mailbox. As soon as you connect, you can read it, reply to it, and so on.

Although you may come to expect certain computers on the Internet to be connected all the time, you should probably assume that most people are actually not connected a fair amount of the time. When they connect, they can interact with other Internet users, such as replying to mail and having interactive sessions. However, for human interaction, the Internet is like the telephone: Many times, we're not near a computer, or we are ignoring the computer.

Getting the Message Across

These pages cover one of the fun technical parts of the Internet that even nontechies enjoy learning. One of the things that makes the Internet so flexible is the way that messages are sent from one place on the Internet to another. The only thing that one computer on the Internet needs to know to be able send a message to another computer is the address of the destination computer. With that address, the originating computer simply plops the message on the Internet, and the message is automatically routed to the destination.

At first, this may seem a bit obvious. For example, when you make a phone call from your home to someone in another city, you don't really care about all the telephone offices through which your call is routed on the way to the other end. However, routing phone calls is trivial relative to routing Internet messages. Every area code is a single geographic location and, within that area code, the first three digits of the telephone number are a single geographic area within the larger area.

Internet addresses don't tell you anything about location. For example, the computer at address "220.27.102.14" may be in one part of the world and the computer at "220.27.102.15" may be in a completely different part of the world, thousands of miles away. This doesn't matter to the computer sending the

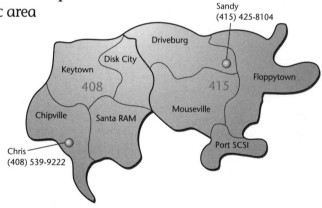

▶ When Chris dials Sandy's telephone number, the local phone company's switching system finds a route to Sandy's area code (415), and from there finds a route to the 425 prefix in Driveburg.

▶ *Assume that your message consists of four parts, pictured here as members of a singing quartet.*

▶ *They are flying from San Jose to Boston, but they didn't plan ahead very well, so the airline had to send them on different routes.*

message, though: It simply puts the message on the Internet and the message is sent to the proper place, automatically.

How Do Addresses Work?

How is this accomplished if the address doesn't indicate a location? The answer lies in the definition of the Internet as a "network of networks." Each address tells you the location of a computer on a network. The address "220.27.102.14" is a computer on a network. All computers on that network have an address that starts with "220.27.102." Thus, to

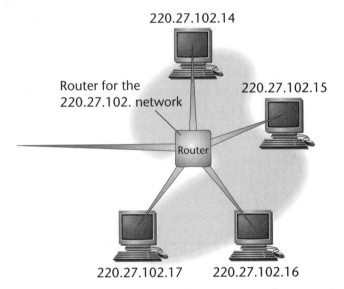

▶ *To get a message to a specific computer, all you need to do is get the message to the router for the network that the destination computer is on. From there, it's the network's responsibility to get the message to the computer.*

get a message to "220.27.102.14," all you really need to do is get the message to the network "220.27.102.0," and let the network take care of it from there.

▶ Along the way, the quartet members go through different cities, which are like routers on the Internet.

Routers

Earlier, you saw that each network on the Internet was connected to other networks using *routers*. Routers do many things, but what they do of most interest to the discussion at hand is that they try to get messages to routers as close to the recipient as possible. Some routers don't do a very good job of this: All they do is send the message to the next biggest router nearby. Other routers, particularly those run by large Internet providers, do a much better job and can reduce the number of routers that a message must go through.

▶ In Boston, they reassemble when the fourth member finally arrives.

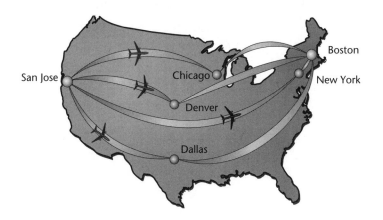

Split Messages

On the way to the destination computer, a message might be split into many parts that are sent along different routes. That's okay as long as the message is reassembled at the destination. This splitting may happen for a variety of reasons, but the reason doesn't really affect users as long as messages always arrive intact.

Messages that are split on the Internet are actually more reliable than our quartet here. For example, if part of a message is lost in transit, the destination computer tells the originating computer and that part of the messsage is sent again. The originating computer can also specify that the message is useless after a certain amount of time and that the destination computer should ignore the message if it has taken too long to get all the parts together.

Getting an Internet Connection

By now, you may be ready to get started and get an account on an Internet-capable machine. If it were as easy as going down to the local computer store and buying a piece of software, you would be all set; but it isn't that easy. You need to make a few decisions first, and then you need to find Internet access providers in your area.

In the back of this book, you'll find a listing of just a few of the hundreds of companies that provide local access to the Internet. Only some area codes are listed, and only some of the providers within each area code are shown. More companies are making access available every day, and you may find that you prefer a tiny mom-and-pop BBS to a large, professional service, or vice versa.

Choosing a Provider

One major decision you'll need to make is whether you want a provider that gives you a simple dial-in (character-based) or one that gives you *SLIP or PPP* service. These are very different kinds of Internet connections, and Internet providers often have different price structures for them. SLIP and PPP, which are ways to connect computers to the Internet over serial lines, are described later in this book. The basic difference between SLIP and PPP and a simple dial-in is that the interface for dial-in systems is not nearly as easy to use.

Free-nets Bulletin board systems connected to the Internet that are free or charge only a nominal amount for use. The idea is to give all the people in a community free access to computing and to information on the Internet. Free-nets are usually supported by volunteer staff and local donations.

How Much Access Do You Want?

As you've already read, another major issue is how fully connected to the Internet your service provider is. If you connect to a small BBS, you may get only electronic mail exchange. Many BBSs now also offer Usenet news, and a few offer a complete package of Internet services. Most companies that advertise themselves as Internet connections offer all the Internet services such as World Wide Web, Gopher, telnet, and so on; however, they may not offer anything else, such as the local feel of a small BBS.

How Much Do You Want to Spend?

Of course, cost is also a consideration. Some services charge by the hour, others let you use their services as much as you want for a flat rate per month. Many services have different prices during different parts of the day. Others have a combination of both: up to a certain number of hours for a fixed cost, and an additional charge per hour after that.

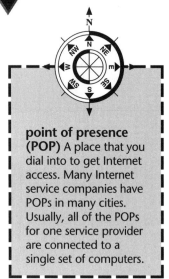

point of presence (POP) A place that you dial into to get Internet access. Many Internet service companies have POPs in many cities. Usually, all of the POPs for one service provider are connected to a single set of computers.

This is one of the most confusing parts of choosing an Internet connection because it's likely that the service providers in your area will have different pricing structures. If you are just starting to browse the Internet and don't have a clear picture of what you want to do, you may be better off choosing a service that has a low monthly minimum and charges by the hour. If you're pretty sure you'll be an addicted Internaut fairly quickly, you'll want to start with a service that has a flat fee.

Is There a Local POP?

The location of your Internet service's modems is called *point of presence* or *POP*. Some large providers have many POPs throughout the country, while most small companies have only one POP. When you choose a provider, you want to be sure you choose a POP that is as close as possible to you so that you can avoid accumulating big phone bills from using the POP.

One advantage of smaller Internet providers is that the POP is usually in the same location as the main Internet computer, and that's also where people work. If something goes wrong with the hardware in the POP (and we all know how often things go wrong with hardware), people are right there to fix it. Most large providers that have dozens of POPs don't have people at the site, so it might take hours to get the POP working again. On the other hand, the large service providers are more familiar with the kinds of problems they could have with POP hardware.

Other Considerations

There are many other important considerations when choosing your Internet provider. Some include

- **Service** Getting started with any online service can be difficult, so you want a company that is available to help you. This is particularly true for SLIP and PPP connections, which are notoriously hard to set up on your personal computer.

- **Reliability** If the provider has computer or phone problems, you can't access the Internet when you want to.

- **Local feeling** The Internet spans the globe, but you often will want to chat with people in your own town. Some Internet services have additional features that let you talk to local people.

- **Closeness** Depending on how your phone company bills for local calls, the actual location of the provider's modems might be very important to keeping your phone bills down.

SLIP (Serial Line IP) and PPP (Point-to-Point Protocol) Fast and reliable methods for connecting computers on the Internet over serial lines, such as telephone wire. PPP has become more popular than SLIP in the past few years, and many Internet service providers offer PPP connections. Using PPP or SLIP, your personal computer becomes connected directly to the Internet.

The Importance of Choosing Wisely

It is fairly important to choose your Internet providers wisely. After you set up your account on the Internet, you will tell all your friends, relatives, and colleagues your Internet address. If you later decide to change to a different Internet provider, it is difficult to tell everyone your new address, and your old service may not want to forward your e-mail to you.

You should also remember this when choosing your user name when you sign up for your Internet account. Some people choose cute names like "speed-racer" or "net-dude," but later decide they want to have a more professional presence on the Internet. At that point, you are forced to get a second account and end up paying double because of your mistake.

Internet Connections for Business

For many businesses, choosing the kind of Internet connection they want is quite difficult. If you have been in your business for 15 years, you probably remember how hard it was to decide what kind of computers to buy in the early 1980s (and today's computer purchase decisions are still not that easy to make). Businesses choosing how to interact with the Internet today have a similar problem. Commercial use of the Internet is still in its infancy, making long-term decisions about Internet connectivity all the more confusing. Of course, different kinds of businesses will have different needs when it comes to using the Internet.

Deciding to Publish on the Internet

The biggest question that companies, particularly small ones, have to ask (or answer) now is whether or not to advertise (or "publish") on the Internet. You may choose to purchase advertising through a company that already publishes on the Internet. In this case, your own company's Internet connection may not matter, because the existing publisher handles everything for you.

Establishing an Internet Presence

However, there is much more that a company can do to have a presence on the Internet. For example, if your business has a catalog for your customers, you might want to put an electronic edition of the catalog online for everyone to see. In this case, you either need to publish the catalog through someone who has a stable, high-speed connection to the Internet, or you need to get such a connection yourself. If you want to be able to take orders over the Internet, you also have to consider the reliability and security of your Internet service, not just its speed.

Within the next few years, almost every business should have electronic mail for many or all of its workers. E-mail is an incredible business tool for communications within your company, as well as with your clients, suppliers, partners, prospects, and so on. Many companies have found Internet mail to be as valuable as fax systems, and it allows them to cut phone bills significantly while increasing productivity.

Selecting a Connection

Internet connections for businesses come in many styles and speeds. Each type of connection requires different hardware at your company. Most businesses choose to dedicate a single computer (often a PC or a minicomputer) to be the gateway between the business and the Internet, and for most situations this is sufficient. The most popular operating system for Internet connections is UNIX, but the Macintosh, and PCs running Windows NT are becoming popular as well.

Getting the Hardware

Beyond the actual computer, however, you also need to purchase or lease communications hardware for your Internet connection. The communications hardware you use in your company must match the hardware used by your Internet provider. If yours is a small company that primarily uses the Internet for mail and does not publish on the Internet, a low-speed connection with a 28.8 kilobaud *modem* is probably sufficient. You may not even need a dedicated computer for your gateway. If you do require greater speed and reliability in your Internet connection, you will have to choose a different type of technology, probably including a high-speed connection and a dedicated computer.

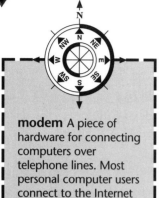

modem A piece of hardware for connecting computers over telephone lines. Most personal computer users connect to the Internet over modems, although some have direct connections through company networks. Most modems cost under $100, although faster modems can cost over $500.

Consult with your Internet provider about what kind of connection you want, what you can afford, and the type of access you can get through your local phone company. For instance, if your company is located in a remote area (or if you have an antiquated phone service), you may not be able to get a high-speed line to your office. However, most Internet providers are quite good at determining how to get you an adequate connection even in such circumstances.

Sharing Connections

Neighboring companies frequently share Internet connections in order to save money. If you are in an office building with other businesses, and another company on your floor has bought an Internet connection, you may be able to "piggyback" onto its connection for much less than it would cost to buy your own. This is a good way for companies just starting out on the Internet to get experience, and it helps both companies by lowering costs.

Internet Connections for Home

Home users have a much easier time choosing an Internet connection than business users. Few home users want to publish on the Internet, so the major concerns are cost and service. Fortunately, there are already many good Internet providers for home users, and the number will certainly grow in the near future.

To access the Internet from home, you need a modem and a personal computer. Almost any modem and PC will do for most services, but the faster the modem you get, the faster you'll get the information you want from the Internet. Today, the fastest modems you can buy run at 28.8 kilobaud, which is 12 times faster than the slowest modems sold, 2400 baud. In the midrange, the most common speed is 14.4 kilobaud. You can find 2400 baud modems for under $50, and many 28.8 kilobaud modems sell for around $250.

Commercial Online Services

After getting a modem and a computer, you need to choose which kind of service you want. There are many choices, but they fall into a few categories: major commercial services such as CompuServe, America Online, or Prodigy that offer Internet connections along with a broad range of other online resources; bulletin board systems (BBSs) with Internet mail connections; and local services whose primary purpose is to provide connections to the Internet.

▶America Online's Internet area describes the kinds of connections you can make from the America Online service to the Internet.

If you are a novice and want lots of support, you are probably best off starting with a service like CompuServe, America Online, or Prodigy. They provide a friendly and easygoing way to explore the Internet, and they offer good support (although it is often slow). Furthermore, it is easy to meet and chat with people on these services who share your interests. On the negative side, services of this type are usually more expensive and are not as technically advanced as some other Internet providers.

Bulletin Board Services

If the only reason you want to connect to the Internet is to send and receive mail, you might prefer to use a local BBS. Many are free and are run as a hobby by the system operator (or sysop). Others are very inexpensive, usually $5 or $10 a month for unlimited use. If you live in a medium-to-large city, you can also find many BBSs that are devoted to specific topics of interest to you.

Direct versus Indirect Connection

Home users who want free rein to explore all of the Internet and who are not afraid of venturing out on their own should probably set up either a direct or an indirect connection with a local Internet service. If you set up an indirect connection (relatively inexpensive and easy to establish), you will be able to access all the standard text resources on the Internet, but you won't be able to access information in other forms, such as video, graphics, and sound recordings. If you establish a direct connection (more expensive and harder to set up), you will be able to access multimedia resources as well as text. A direct connection is also referred to as a SLIP (or PPP) connection, and it requires at least a 14.4 kilobaud modem.

Addresses on the Internet

Two types of things have Internet addresses: computers and people. Computers on the Internet have addresses that make it easy to specify which computer you mean. People who have accounts on a particular computer have an address that is made up of their account name and the name of the computer.

You saw earlier that each computer on the Internet has an IP address that has four numbers and looks like "192.47.9.220." That address, although precise, isn't that useful to we humans who use the Internet. A second method for naming computers, called the *domain name system* or *DNS*, gives computers more easy-to-remember names such as "whitehouse.gov" and "compaq.com."

Domain Name System

The domain name system starts with some standard domains that appear at the far right of a computer's name. The most common domains you will see include "com" for commercial companies and "edu" for colleges and universities; there are also domains for countries, organizations, and other groups.

A computer's name has at least two levels of domain, and each level is separated by a period (or dot). To the left of the top-level domain is another name, possibly more than one name. Each level moving left is a subset of the one to the right. So in the name "jsc.nasa.gov," "jsc" is a subdomain of "nasa," which is a subdomain of "gov."

User Addresses

People's addresses are simply the name of their account on the computer, followed by an "at" sign (@), followed by the name of the computer that they are on. For example, the person whose name is "astronaut" on the computer called "jsc.nasa.gov" has an address of "astronaut@jsc.nasa.gov."

You use people's addresses for sending them electronic mail, which is one of the most common things people do on the Internet. Some people have more than one address, such as if they have accounts on more than one computer, but usually, these people have one address where they prefer to get all their mail.

Note that some people's addresses are not for people at all, but for lists of people. When a message is sent to that address, it gets copied to everyone on the list that is maintained at that computer site. For example, an address such as "staff@admin.mynet.net" might indicate all the people on the computer administrative staff at a company called MyNet. A single letter to that address would be automatically duplicated and put in each person's mailbox.

A Note About Addresses

Don't take the names you see in Internet addresses too seriously. The rules for how you get an address are very, very loose, and some addresses are not what they seem. For example, you may want to send mail to someone at Big Modem Company, but don't assume that the computer address "bigmodem.com" is that company. Depending on the domain, it is easy to get an address that may or may not really be who you are.

This warning is particularly true for users' names. The only person who controls who gets mail sent to a particular name is the administrator of the computer. If you have a friend named Nancy at a company called SunTree System, don't assume that "nancy@suntree.com" is the person you want: It could be another Nancy. She might be "nancyt@suntree.com," or she might not even have a mail account on that system, and instead be "nancy@pubs.ny.suntree.com."

To whet your appetite, here are some real addresses of interesting computers on the Internet:

▶ **www.microsoft.com** is the computer that serves as Microsoft's World Wide Web server.

▶ **compuserve.com** is the computer that receives all of the Internet mail that is sent to CompuServe users.

▶ **rtfm.mit.edu** is a system at MIT that holds thousands of files that answer the most-asked questions in Usenet news groups.

Of course, many well-known, interesting people are on the Internet as well. One big-name personality includes **president@whitehouse.gov**, the President of the United States.

Clients and Servers

One of the more popular buzzwords in the computer industry today, *client/server*, is at the heart of most Internet programs. Client/server means different things to different people, but it generally refers to pairs of programs that interact over a network. On the Internet, most of the interesting information is available through programs that are based on the client/server model.

Understanding the Terminology

The important thing to understand about client/server programs is that there are two separate programs. You, the Internet user, run client programs; computers on the Internet that are willing to give you information run server programs. The server program expects requests for information to

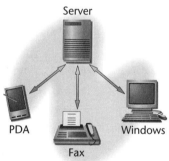

▶ *There can be many clients for one kind of server. This makes the best content on the Internet more accessible to more people.*

**client/server soft-
ware** Software that is
split between two
programs: clients and
servers. The term
client/server has
become widely used in
the computer industry
to describe database
and information retrieval
systems where the user
runs a program on his
or her personal com-
puter that interacts with
a database program on
a host computer.

be given in a particular format; the server then answers requests in a particular format. The client
program knows how to form requests in the manner
that the server wants, as well as how to display the
request to you in a format you like.

Benefiting from the Client/Server Model

You may wonder why there isn't just one program
instead of two to do the job. The beauty of the
client/server model is that it enables you to create
many different client programs that all talk to a
single server. For example, if the server is a mail
server, you might run one client program when you
are getting mail on your personal computer and then
run a very different program when you are getting
mail via your tiny personal digital assistant. The two
programs look and feel different to you, but they work
the same as far as the server is concerned.

The client/server model works great with the Internet because
clients send messages to servers, and servers send messages back to
clients. Message passing is the Internet's strong point. Also, because
the Internet was designed to work with almost any computer, the
client/server model is handy since a server doesn't need to know
what kind of computer the client program is running on.

If the client/server model wasn't used on the Internet, Internet
users would need to know much more to accomplish the things they
want. With client/server, though, if you want to let many people
know about your company, you can structure the information for a
single server. Then, people with a wide variety of client programs
can look at it. As an information provider, you don't have to know
about all the client software out there, just the server.

Advantages on the Client Side

This also makes it easier for people to write great-looking client software. People who are good at writing information-providing programs (servers) don't need to learn about graphical user interfaces (GUIs) in order to make good software. Likewise, people who are good at writing software for personal computers, such as PCs running Windows or Macintosh computers, don't need to know about how to write for the computers that provide the information on the Internet.

Advantages on the Server Side

The split between client and server software also works to the advantage of the people who write the server software. Server software on the Internet usually evolves much more slowly than client software, but when server software changes, it usually changes in a big way. This is because the most popular servers are controlled by standards organizations, which are notoriously slow movers. When a new version of server software is developed, it is specifically designed so that all of the old client software will work with it, but that revised clients will have more capabilities. The split between client and server software lets developers of each move at their own speeds.

client program
A program that a user runs to interface with server software. Client software often looks different on each computer it runs on, taking on the best features of that computer. Many different client programs can interact with one server program.

server program The program that a host computer runs that communicates with users running client programs. Server software establishes a standard for communication, and all client programs must act in that standard fashion in order to work properly. Many different client programs can interact with one server program.

Character-Based and Graphical Clients

When you interact with the Internet, you are always interacting through client programs. Many different client programs exist for each kind of Internet service. Each client runs on a particular kind of computer. Your Internet service may let you choose only one particular client for each type of server, or you may have many choices.

Character-Based Clients

The two broad classes of client programs are character-based and graphical. Historically, almost every type of server started with character-based clients. The longer these clients have been around, the more entrenched they have become. A good example of this is the character-based mail program, unimaginatively called "mail." Even though it uses a command-line interface with cryptic one-character commands, it is still used by a large percentage of the people on the Internet. And, even though better character-based mail clients have been around for years — such as the "elm" and "pine" programs — people are still taught to use the more difficult "mail" program. With a character-based program such as elm, you can select letters to read by typing in their numbers or by using the arrow keys on your keyboard. To give commands, however, you must type a letter, some of which are shown at the bottom of the screen.

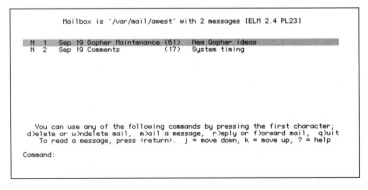

```
        Mailbox is '/var/mail/awest' with 2 messages [ELM 2.4 PL23]

  N  1   Sep 19 Gopher Maintenance (61)   New Gopher ideas
  N  2   Sep 19 Comments            (17)   System timing




    You can use any of the following commands by pressing the first character;
  d)elete or u)ndelete mail,  m)ail a message,  r)eply or f)orward mail,  q)uit
    To read a message, press <return>.  j = move down, k = move up, ? = help

  Command:
```

▶ *The elm program is a popular character-based mail client.*

Because the Internet was formed before the days of Microsoft Windows and Macintosh programs, there is still a strong orientation toward only programs that display characters on a screen exactly 80 characters wide by 24 lines long. In the past few years, many client programs that use graphical interfaces have appeared and in many ways have helped generate interest in the Internet.

Graphical Clients

With a graphical program such as Windows-based Eudora, you select letters to read using the mouse or the keyboard. Like other Windows programs, the commands are all in the program's menu bar. Other advantages of using a graphical program like Eudora is that you can drag messages from one mailbox to another and make choices using icons.

If your connection to the Internet is through SLIP or PPP, two communications protocols that I mentioned earlier, you will almost definitely be using graphical programs. SLIP and PPP essentially put your personal computer on the Internet itself, and therefore the clients use the native features of your operating system. You don't have to use SLIP or PPP to get graphical client programs, but it is currently the most popular way.

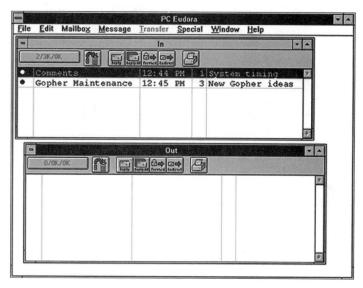

▶ Eudora is a good example of a graphical Internet mail program for Windows.

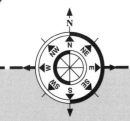

c shell The most common user interface for people whose Internet providers run on character-based UNIX systems. The c shell is also one of the oldest user interfaces still widely used — and it shows. Unless you are a computer weenie, it is unlikely that you will like using the c shell much.

shell A program that allows a user to interact with an operating system. Programs like the MS-DOS command line and Microsoft Windows are shells to the MS-DOS operating system. Under UNIX, there are many popular shells, such as the c shell, Bourne shell, and so on.

Don't feel bad if your Internet provider is still using character-based programs: They work, they are usually reliable, and many have halfway-decent user interfaces. On the other hand, if you are a Macintosh or Windows user and you have a choice between character-based and graphical, you may find using graphical clients easier and more natural.

UNIX and Why Not to Learn It

Until a few years ago, if you wanted access to anything other than just e-mail on the Internet, you had to use a computer based on the UNIX operating system. Mind you, nothing is inherently wrong with UNIX, but it has earned a reputation for being hard to use, cryptic, and just plain unfriendly.

Where Did UNIX Come From?

UNIX was designed by computer geeks for computer geeks, and it shows. The names of commands are all shorter than they have to be (like "cp" for copy and "mv" for move) so that you can type them faster. UNIX's power features can leave even smart computer professionals scratching their heads and searching for the manual.

It doesn't have to be that way. A system administrator on a UNIX computer can make it as easy or as hard to use as he or she wants. Unfortunately, they usually leave the standard method of interaction (called the *c shell*) as the only choice for most users. Learning to use the c shell is not impossible, but it certainly is not for the faint of heart.

Just how bad is the character-based UNIX command line? Well, here's a little pop quiz. Try matching the names of the common UNIX commands on the left with their actions on the right. If you haven't used UNIX before, you can expect to get a zero on this one!

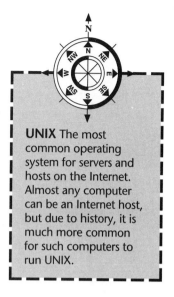

UNIX The most common operating system for servers and hosts on the Internet. Almost any computer can be an Internet host, but due to history, it is much more common for such computers to run UNIX.

UNIX command		Action	
1)	ls	a)	Edit a text file
2)	grep	b)	Print a file
3)	more	c)	Find text in a file
4)	lp	d)	Run a command later
5)	vi	e)	Display the directory
6)	rm	f)	Display a file on the screen
7)	at	g)	Delete a file

Answer key: 1 = e; 2 = c; 3 = f; 4 = b; 5 = a; 6 = g; 7 = d

Alternatives to UNIX

Today, many systems have different interfaces, mostly to help beginning users who want to use the standard Internet services and not have to learn any UNIX. If you are using SLIP or PPP to access the Internet, you don't have to worry about seeing UNIX, ever. If you have a dial-in account, the interface you see depends on what your access provider chooses. If it insists on giving you UNIX and you don't feel comfortable with it, you might want to find a different provider.

If you are forced to learn a bit of UNIX to get access to the Internet, you should ask your provider what the least you might need to learn is. If the provider is your school or company, it may offer courses in "just enough UNIX" that will get you through the beginnings. There are also many books for UNIX novices that should help you learn enough to learn the part you really want: accessing the Internet.

CERT (Computer Emergency Response Team) A security force for the Internet. CERT is a clearinghouse of information about network security, known security problems on the Internet, and attempted (or successful) break-ins. It has an FTP site that has definitive versions of common Internet server software.

Internet Security

If the Internet were like a small town, we could all leave our houses' and cars' doors unlocked knowing that they would be safe and all would be okay when we came back. Needless to say, that's not the case. However, many Internet users (in fact, many computer users) don't understand what they can do to help make the information on their computers more secure in a hostile environment.

Why You Should Think About Security

If you're not sure why you should be concerned with security, consider the following two scenarios that are taken from real-world stories:

- Gary, an employee of Giant Publishing, wants to find out what's going on at Fantastic Books, a competing company. Gary knows that his old friend, Dan, has an account on Fantastic Books' internal computer system, and he also knows that Dan really likes football. Gary determines Dan's login name, starts guessing at local football players' names as Dan's password, and gets into Dan's account. Gary then runs many programs that tell him about future projects, management changes, and so on.

- Gary also has a grudge against Penny and wants to humiliate her. Using the same techniques as he did with Dan, he logs into Penny's account and looks through her personal files, such as the copies of mail people have sent to her. He then sends out dozens of letters that appear to be from her, saying derogatory things, but in a tone that is believable. Penny gets astonished replies from some of the people, but doesn't know who else might have gotten such mail, and has no idea how it was sent in the first place.

Choosing a Password

The most important thing to remember is that your password is your best, and often your only, defense against attack. In order to be safe, you must choose a password that no one else can guess. Also, you should not give your password to anyone, not even people whom you are sure won't hurt you, because they may accidentally give out your password to someone who will use it against you.

Each Internet provider has different rules about passwords. Some let you choose your own, while others provide them for you. It's a good idea to change your password often in case someone has guessed it but has not yet used it against you in a way you can tell. Remember, the more obscure the password, the less likely someone else will guess it.

The situation with security on the Internet is unfortunate but very real. For every article you read about in the newspaper, hundreds or thousands of other incidents occur that you'll never hear about. Most societies are built on some level of trust, but in a society as wide as the Internet's, you should seriously consider the kind of trust you want to give to so many strangers.

Electronic Frontier Foundation (EFF) one of the first large groups concerned with Internet-related privacy and access issues. The EFF educates and lobbies extensively in Washington, D.C., and often teaches local law enforcement agencies how computer technology is — and is not — like other issues with which they are familiar. The EFF is one of the strongest supporters of personal freedoms on the Internet.

netiquette A play on the word etiquette: the proper way to behave on the Internet. This includes respecting the rights and desires of others, setting an example of how you want strangers to treat you, and acknowledging that the Internet is very different than face-to-face communication.

Netiquette

Like every society, the Internet has often-unspoken rules of conduct. Some of the customs are common sense, such as treating each other as well as you would like to be treated, while others are more arcane, such as using abbreviations instead of spelling out common phrases. If you want to fit in well with other Internet users, you'll want to pay attention to the feeling of the interactions that are already common before you try to set your own tone.

What Is Netiquette?

The Internet's social rules, which are called *netiquette*, developed when the Internet had few people and the bandwidth was more limited. These rules are also based on the fact that the Internet is an international meeting place, and most people are unaware of local customs in other countries. Now that the Internet is growing rapidly, it seems likely that the rules will probably shift a bit and be easier to grasp for the millions of new users.

Most of the common netiquette guidelines cover human-to-human interactions, such as on mailing lists and in Usenet news groups. Others, however, cover how to be good Internet citizens with respect to using Internet resources. For example, copying files from computers halfway across the globe just because you are not being charged for it is not a good use of limited resources. It is good to not forget that you shouldn't do something just because no one will notice if you do; remember that everything you do on the Internet has repercussions, even if your actions can't be traced back to you.

Some Basic Rules

Some of the more common rules of netiquette include

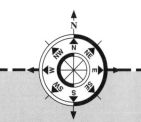

- Many people subscribe to mailing lists or read Usenet news groups without ever posting. When you post a message, remember that there may be 10 or 100 times as many people reading it as you think.

- Take responsibility for what you say. Don't hide behind the Internet's anonymity because this weakens the social bond on the Internet as a whole.

- When someone says something that strikes you as odd, consider the fact that you probably have no idea who they are, where they grew up, or what kind of society that they live in. "bill@netservice.net" might live in California, Arkansas, Germany, India, or Ghana — or next door to you and have moved from any of those places last week.

- Don't say anything in public that you wouldn't want your child, your mother, or your boss to see. Before reacting hastily to something that someone else has said, take three deep breaths and ask yourself whether an angry blast or flame is the best way to respond.

flame To attack someone in a discussion, usually with language much harsher than necessary. Flames are usually personal even when the flamer is attacking ideas. The term comes from the concept of a heated debate.

PART 3

Internet Information Services

For most people, the best part of the Internet is all the information you can get from it and the interesting people you can meet. In order to find these things, however, you have to know how information is arranged on the Internet. This section shows you all the wonderful Internet services, most of which are free, so you can then delve deeper into each one.

Mail

The most popular form of communication on the Internet is electronic mail. This form of communication is so ubiquitous today on every computer network that it isn't even necessary to call it electronic mail or e-mail: it's just mail. Paper mail will probably be with us forever, but its usefulness is rapidly diminishing in colleges and companies, and even between friends. Someday, mail may mean electronic mail for most things and paper mail for advertising.

Mail is a basic feature of the Internet; it's also very easy to use. As you saw earlier, every person with an account on a computer on the

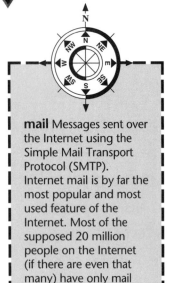

mail Messages sent over the Internet using the Simple Mail Transport Protocol (SMTP). Internet mail is by far the most popular and most used feature of the Internet. Most of the supposed 20 million people on the Internet (if there are even that many) have only mail access.

Internet has a mail address, and sending mail to someone is as easy as remembering their address and typing. Dozens of mail client programs for different computers are available and, because mail is such a popular use of the Internet, these programs are becoming more powerful and easier to use every day.

Don't think of Internet mail as just for businesses. It is an excellent way to keep in touch with friends who are more than a local call away. This type of mail is also a good method for saying something short — a postcard's worth — and sending it off instead of waiting for enough news to justify writing a long letter. Internet e-mail has also helped hundreds of thousands of people stay in touch with old friends after they move.

Advantages of Electronic Mail

If you haven't used Internet mail, you may be skeptical of how much better it is than paper mail. Some of the many advantages of Internet mail include

▶ **Instant delivery:** Well, almost instant. Mail within a single network usually takes only a few seconds to be delivered. The time it takes to send mail across the continent varies, but messages that travel thousands of miles often arrive in under a minute, depending on how jammed the Internet is and how busy the sending and receiving computers are.

▶ **Easy organization:** You can store messages in files that are similar to folders used for paper messages. The advantage of these files is that you can quickly find an old message you're looking for by searching through the text of the file to find a key word. Another Internet-mail feature is the ability to save a message in many different files at once, such as having one file for all messages from a particular person and one file for all messages on a particular subject.

▶ **Intelligent replies:** Have you ever received a letter that says, "On the point you made in the second paragraph, I disagree" without it saying which letter and which point? Most mail-client programs make it easy for you to include the exact text that you are discussing in your reply, thereby decreasing the chance of a misunderstanding.

▶ **Group letters:** You can type a message once and send it to many people without having to type it again (or, in the case of

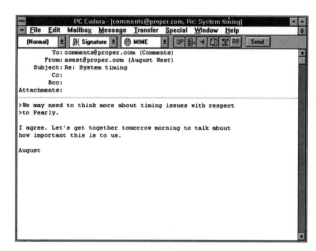

▶ *This message is a reply. Every line that begins with a ">" symbol is text from the original letter. The person replying didn't have to type any of this. After reading the original message, they simply gave a single command and the mail program prepared this reply for easy editing.*

paper mail, photocopying it). For example, if you are preparing a group presentation, you can create a small mailing list of everyone in the group and send a message to that list: you don't even need to remember who is in the group.

Using Electronic Mail

Although creating electronic mail is no easier than regular mail (you still have to type, after all), replying to electronic mail is significantly easier. Most mail client programs have a "Reply" command that automatically addresses a response to the person who sent you the letter you are reading. These programs also often have a "Forward" command that allows you to copy the letter that you just got to someone else. For example, if a coworker sends you an announcement for an upcoming workshop, and you know that someone else

would be interested in that workshop, you simply select the "Forward" command, enter the new person's mail address, and the message is instantly duplicated to them.

The Changing Face of Communications

Internet mail has already changed the way that many companies and university professors work. It vastly reduces the cost of international telephone calls and makes it easy for people in distant time zones to communicate during their own business hours. Although faxes helped start this trend, they are more expensive (and much less convenient) than Internet mail.

Using this type of mail also changes the way you communicate, in the same way that the telephone changed the way people communicated compared with paper mail. It is much easier to whip off a three-sentence message using Internet mail than it is to write a short letter, address the envelope, and pay the postage. Two people can send a series of five or six messages back and forth in a single day at almost no cost. For many reasons, Internet mail probably has increased the number of brief communications among the people who use it.

MIME The standard for enclosing binary files in Internet mail. MIME, which stands for Multipurpose Internet Mail Extensions, lets you specify the type of attachment you are making to your Internet mail. Many nonmail programs, such as the World Wide Web, also use MIME so client programs can more easily read files.

encryption The process of scrambling a message so that it is virtually impossible for someone else to read without the key. Encryption maintains privacy when sending messages and also verifies the sender's identity. The Internet uses many different kinds of encryption, and none of them are compatible with each other.

Managing Your Mail

Most mail client programs also let you file your mail in a fashion similar to the way you use paper files. However, because electronic mail is so easy to copy (and usually takes up only a small amount of disk space), you can duplicate the message into as many files as you want. For instance, assume that you got a letter from Helene with a question about a particular client. Before filing the message, you would duplicate it and put one copy in the folder for your correspondence with Helene and another copy in the folder for your correspondence about that client.

World Wide Web

The recent surge in media coverage of the Internet has focused on new Internet services instead of tried-and-true ones, such as mail. The service that has caught the press's eye the most is the *World Wide Web*, or the Web for short. The Web works well with graphical user interfaces — such as Windows and the Macintosh — and many people think that the Web is thus easier to use than other services.

Accessing the Web

Using the Web is, in fact, easy. You can use a mouse for pointing and clicking to take you to different information on the Web, to move around from host to host on the Internet, and to view graphics files (if you have patience). The two most common client software programs for the Web are NCSA Mosaic and Netscape; however, there are dozens of other programs that also access the Web. Even without the graphics, the Web is quite attractive because you can see formatted text with things such as boldface, different fonts, and colors.

The Web, however, is not a universal panacea for the Internet. It is just one service, and even with its advanced interface, it has many limitations. One of the biggest limitations is that it is primarily a one-way medium: there are very few places on the Web where you can interact with anything more than a search command. Although this is not an inherent limitation of the structure of the

World Wide Web (WWW) An Internet service that lets users retrieve hypertext and graphics from various sites. Often just called "the Web," this has become one of the most popular Internet services in the past two years. In fact, many Internet information providers publish using only the Web.

HTML (Hypertext Markup Language) The formatting language World Wide Web servers use. HTML documents are text files with commands imbedded in them.

SLIP (Serial Line IP) A fast, simple method for connecting computers on the Internet over serial lines, such as telephone wire. PPP has become more popular than SLIP in the past few years, although many Internet service providers offer SLIP connections as well as PPP connections. Using PPP or SLIP, your personal computer is connected directly to the Internet.

PPP (Point-to-Point Protocol) A fast, reliable method for connecting computers on the Internet over serial lines, such as telephone wire. PPP has become more popular than SLIP in the past few years, and many Internet service providers offer PPP connections. Using PPP or SLIP, your personal computer becomes directly connected to the Internet.

▶ Many companies now use the Web for more than just advertising. Compaq, for example, offers technical support and customer service through its Web site.

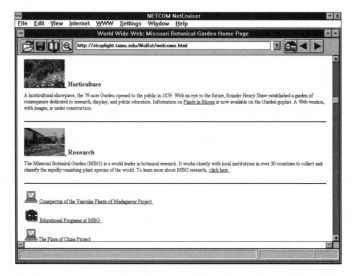

▶ If you are on a fast Internet link, or you have a lot of patience, you can find many beautiful pictures on the Web. There are dozens of art galleries, museums, and other visually delightful areas.

Web, people on the Internet seem to like interactive services, such as mail and Usenet news, a lot more than ones where you mostly look at screens of information.

This is not to say that there isn't great information on the Web, or that it isn't at all interactive. Because you can view graphics easily (if slowly), information that is mostly graphical such as art collections, maps, photographs, and so on can be arranged easily on the Web. And some sites, particularly commercial sites, have been using the Web's interactive features to allow you to place orders for merchandise online.

Using Hypertext

The Web's strongest asset is its use of hypertext, which is text or pictures that are linked to other documents. Within a hypertext document, some text is highlighted to indicate that clicking on it will lead you to somewhere else. This link might be to another part of the same document, or to a different document on the same computer, or to a document somewhere else altogether.

Interacting with Other Services

Another great feature of Web clients is that they can do more than just read Web documents: they can also interact with other Internet services. With most Web clients — such as Mosaic or Netscape — you can also display Gopher documents, start telnet sessions, send mail to people, get files by anonymous FTP, and so on. This makes the Web a good collecting place for resources all over the Internet.

lynx A character-based client program for the World Wide Web. Although lynx is not as flashy as other Web clients such as Mosaic, it works well for the millions of Internet users who have only character-based access.

Mosaic A graphical client program for the World Wide Web. To use Mosaic, you must have a direct (SLIP or PPP) connection to the Internet. Even though only a small minority of users today have a direct Internet connection, Mosaic has contributed a great deal to the Internet's recent surge in popularity.

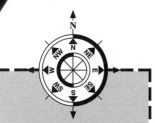

hypertext Documents that contain links to other documents. When reading a hypertext document, you can quickly jump to linked documents and then jump back when you feel like it. Hypertext lets you organize the information you read into different formats.

The link that is about to be selected

PC-related Gophers and WWW servers

If you are new to using the Internet, you might want to read general descriptions of <u>Gopher</u> and <u>World Wide Web</u> (<u>WWW</u>). You may also be interested in a general text description of the <u>PC Gopher and WWW servers</u>.

There are many Gopher servers relating to the PC:

- <u>IBM Kiosk for Education (Gopher)</u>
- <u>IBM Almaden Research Center</u>

<u>Microsoft</u> maintains a server that has some information that is not on their anonymous FTP server. They will probably add much more Web-specific content to their server over time.

Both the <u>IBM Kiosk for Education</u> and the <u>IBM Almaden Research Center</u> are also available as Web servers. IBM has a new <u>centralized IBM Web server</u> that they are still getting the kinks out of, but is a good place to start looking for IBM information.

A new information provider, <u>PC Lube and Tune</u>, has many interesting articles on PCs and networking issues. The articles are updated often, and are usually quite detailed. The name of the service comes from yet-another-extension of the overused "information highway" metaphor.

If you use a <u>Novell</u> network, you may be interested in their server, which has lots of technical notes and marketing information. <u>Farallon</u>, another network hardware and software manufacturer, also has an excellent Web server. Other PC-related manufacturers with Web servers include <u>QuarterDeck Office Systems</u>, <u>MathWorks</u>, <u>Global Village Communications</u>, and <u>Spyglass</u>.

<u>Ziff Davis</u>, publishers of many magazines such as PC Magazine and PC Week, have a new World Wide Web server. Currently, it has only some of PC Week's reviews and such, but it looks like they will be adding to it in the future.

▶ *Hypertext links are great ways of quickly finding the information you want. To get from the document you are viewing to another document, simply click on the link to that document.*

Exit 130.132

Fuel	Service
Advice	Education
Honesty	Directions

PC Lube & Tune

Welcome to PC Lube and Tune

Recent changes to PCLT are noted in our newspaper, "<u>Road and Hack</u>."

PC Lube and Tune is a Service Station and convenience store at Exit 130.132 on the National Information Highway. An ordinary Service Station provides gas, sodas, repairs, maps, and advice. The PCLT <u>objective</u> is to supply usable introductions, tutorials, and education on technical subjects to the large audience of computer users. The <u>method</u> is to supply system independent hypertext files using the tools of the Internet World Wide Web project.

If you have a problem with links, the correct, complete reference to PCLT is

 <u>http://pclt.cis.yale.edu/pclt/default.htm</u> .

▶ *This is what you see after following the previous link.*

Publishing on the Web

Many Internet service providers are letting their customers put up their own information on the World Wide Web. This means that you can publish your writing or art, or just list other interesting things on the Internet that you have found. If your provider lets you do this, consider that hundreds of thousands of people might look at your work. How do you want to present yourself? What kind of things would you say to perfect strangers that you think they might find interesting or useful? Should you include graphics or just use text? Should you have someone else edit your work so that it reads better? As you can see, publishing on the World Wide Web involves difficult decisions and should not be taken lightly.

Unfortunately, to use the graphical parts of the Web, you currently need a SLIP or PPP account, or a direct connection to the Internet. People with character-based connections can still see the text of the Web using a character-based Web client called

Items that look like this are links to other documents.

▶ *This is a typical screen from the Web. It has a few graphics to spice things up a bit, and lots of links to click on.*

Items that look like this are links to other documents.

▶ *This is the same page as the previous one, but in the text-based lynx Web browser. Note that all the important information is here, but it isn't nearly as pretty.*

Areas for you to type in text

Choose one item from a predetermined list with your mouse

○ CD-ROM

○ Windows (diskette)

○ Kid's Education (diskette)

○ Games (diskette)

○ Desk Top Publishing (diskette)

○ DOS Programs (diskette)

Credit card type: ○ VISA ○ Mastercard ○ Discover ○ AMEX

[_____] - Credit Card Number

[_____] - Name on the Card

[_____] - Expiration (MM/YY)

[_____] - Any additional instructions?

▶ *Most of the commercial services that are starting to sprout on the Internet use the Web as their interface. Using forms such as this on the Web, you can fill out information about yourself, and even order products using a credit card or some other type of preauthorization.*

lynx, but it just isn't the same. Popular graphic-based Web clients (sometimes called Web browsers) include Mosaic and Netscape.

In the future, even more services will be available on the Web. Companies are creating Web clients that include user authentication (so you can prove who you are), encryption (so you can send private messages), and many other advanced features. Given how much press the Web is getting, it will be the hotbed for Internet development for many years.

Gopher

Gopher is a very popular Internet service that leads you to information on all sorts of subjects. Although not as flashy as the World Wide Web, more people use it because it works quite well with the still-popular character-based systems. Even though the Web gets almost all the press, more people access more useful information off of Gopher than off of the Web (although that may change soon).

Using Gopher Menus

Instead of using hypertext as the Web does, Gopher uses a simpler concept: menus. Each item in Gopher is either a menu or a file. All Gopher clients show you the difference between the two. Gopher can retrieve many kinds of files, such as text, sound, program, and so on.

Like on the Web, entries in a Gopher menu can take you to computers far away from the one you are on at the moment. Some Gopher menus are lists of other Gopher menus, but most lead you to related information on a particular host computer.

An example screen for what you'll get when you use Gopher to peruse Oxford University's library.

Visiting Gopherspace

You can visit hundreds of interesting places in Gopherspace. Because of its roots at the University of Minnesota, many Gopher servers are at universities. Although a few college-based Gopher servers restrict access to only the people at their school, most allow anyone to go in and peruse their offerings. They list everything from the contents of the college library to course catalogs, books, and thousands of other kinds of information.

Oxford University's library is among the many places that have made hundreds of books available on the Internet. Some U.S. Internet sites also have collections of books and technical manuals that you can read or download.

Using Gopher is quite easy. When you connect to part of a Gopher server, you are presented with a menu that contains the titles of other menus and/or the titles of documents you can view. You simply choose the title you want and click on it, which takes you to the desired menu or, if you chose a document, shows you the document.

▶ Many colleges have centralized all their public information into Gopher servers.

Client software for Gopher is becoming less common because client software for the Web can also interact with Gopher just as well. Thus, instead of having to run

Online PC publications

   📄 <u>Overview of online publications</u>

   📄 <u>Description of the PC publications</u>

   📄 <u>ASP Shareware Catalog for BBS Users</u>

   📁 <u>The Online World book</u>

   📄 <u>Windows Programmer's Journal</u>

   📄 <u>Game Bytes, no graphics (~1 megabyte)</u>

   📄 <u>Game Bytes, with graphics (~1.3 megabytes)</u>

   📄 <u>GeoBytes Newsletter (must have GeoWorks to view)</u>

   📁 <u>Frequently asked question files (FAQs)</u>

▶ *Gopher menus are always presented as lists of choices. A menu can list other menus or files that you can look at or download to your personal computer.*

Gopher A menu-based service that lets you easily find information on all kinds of subjects. Gopher presents all information as either a directory or a file, and most Gopher servers let you search for information as well. More than 1,000 Gopher servers are available on the Internet, and Gopher client programs exist for almost every computer.

Veronica A service that searches for files on Gopher servers. You use a Gopher client to access a Veronica server, then send Veronica a search request. Veronica servers can give you answers in a variety of ways, such as by listing only directories that match your request.

one program for the Web and one program for Gopher, you can just run your Web program and still access all of the services on Gopher.

Usenet Newsgroups

Internet mail is great for chatting with another person, or a small group of people, but it doesn't work well with larger groups. Thousands of mailing lists exist, but individual discussions on mailing lists are hard to follow. When many people want to talk about a particular topic, a different structure is needed.

More than ten years ago, a group of people tried to remedy this situation by creating a method where news on particular topics was passed around from computer to computer. That system, *Usenet*, eventually merged with the Internet, and now all Usenet messages are passed over the Internet. Usenet serves as the structure for discussions that have particular themes.

Like many things on the Internet, Usenet is a barely controlled anarchy. Anyone can read from and post to any of the groups. Although you cannot create just any group you want anywhere, there is a section for groups where you can. And other people can destroy what you create. For most of Usenet, the level of discourse stays reasonable, but there are many Usenet areas where everything from the weird to the profane is part of daily life.

Usenet Hierarchies

Usenet is a collection of *newsgroups*. Each group is part of a hierarchy. The groups have names that match their hierarchies and the topic discussed is usually somewhat related to the name. For example, the horse enthusiast newsgroup, "rec.equestrian," is part of the *rec.* hierarchy, which discusses recreation.

The major Usenet hierarchies are

▶ **alt.** everything under the sun (uncontrolled)

▶ **bit.** duplicates of some mailing lists

▶ **comp.** computers and networks

▶ **k12.** education

▶ **misc.** not easily categorized (controlled)

▶ **news.** Usenet itself

▶ **rec.** recreation (sports, games, pets)

Usenet A widely-used Internet service that organizes people's comments by topic. These topics, called newsgroups, have their own structure, with people commenting on previous comments and starting new discussions. Usenet is the second most popular Internet feature, after mail.

newsgroups Topical divisions of Usenet. A newsgroup generally has a single topic (for example, communications software for Microsoft Windows), but anyone can ask or answer questions. The term "news" is outdated: the majority of the discussion in newsgroups has to do with old items, not news.

thread In a Usenet newsgroup, a chain of postings on a single subject.

▶ **sci.** science and health

▶ **soc.** society and cultures

▶ **talk.** general chatting, some political

Each hierarchy may contain many levels. For example, if you're interested in games for the PC, you would look in the group "comp.sys.ibm.pc.games." Under *comp.*, one of the hierarchies is *sys.* for computer systems. *ibm* is, well, IBM. *pc.* indicates that the systems are not mainframes; and then you finally get to the real discussion, *games.*

You cannot create new Usenet newsgroups of your own without following some fairly strict rules. A major exception to this is the *alt.* hierarchy, where most rules are meant to be broken, although even *alt.* has some rules.

-	Andrew J. Ger...	Wanted: Any MSG fri or sat extras
-	GrDead94	Looking for Chicago 93 & 94 tapes
▽ 3	Joshua Bardwell	Dead Dreams / Skeleton Key
	Shmogger	Re: Dead Dreams / Skeleton Key
	Mike Stillman	Re: Dead Dreams / Skeleton Key
	Edmobo	Re: CALVIN/HOBBES/DEAD CITING
	Marty Lindower	Re: MSG FINALLY!!!
	Hal Broome	Susan James/Jefferson Starship @ Mountain Winery, Sept. 16 '94
-	AGrtflDve	Encores
▽ 2	Juzer T. Kopti	Grateful Dead tix, Wash DC, Oct 9
	Jim McVey	Re: Grateful Dead tix, Wash DC, Oct 9
	Mike - Grobelch	Shoreline Sunday, 9/18/94
	Ethan S Yunger...	Dead hourin Pitt.
	schwartz	Boston or MSG Tix
▽ 2	Mike Dobbs	Billy's arm - Egypt '78?
	PIGGAR714	Re: Billy's arm - Egypt '78?
	BlakPeter	It's just bugging me...
▽ 4	BlakPeter	Europe or Dead... any thoughts?
	skay@polsci.u...	Re: Europe or Dead... any thoughts?
	Sean E. Kutzko	Re: Europe or Dead... any thoughts?
	Marcus Thunich	Re: Europe or Dead... any thoughts?
	Caratunk	Officer Obe has died
▽ 2	Jim McVey	Re: setlist [Sep 17, 1994]
	John A Lescisin	Re: setlist [Sep 17, 1994]
	Shel Holtz	9-18-94 Shoreline Setlist
	Sweeney99	Samson & Delilah chords/lyrics needed
	thunderbolt	clemintine rocks
	barbara lewis	9/6/69 Family Day question
▽ 2	Rob Hermann	Boston tickets for sale

▶ *Notice that many topics are being discussed in this group. Each thread has its own subject name, and some have many responses, but others have just a few (or none yet).*

Discussion Threads

Within each newsgroup, there are *threads* of discussion. When someone posts a new message, it starts a thread. People can reply to the message, which continues the thread. At any one time, there may be dozens of discussion threads happening at once. It is somewhat like listening to all the conversations at a large party at the same time.

programs make it easy to follow threads. When you check the newsgroup, the program collects all the items on that thread into one clump...

The beginning...

Out of the thousands of Usenet newsgroups, where would you...? That depends completely on what you find interesting. For example, "soc.culture.japan" is a very active group, but if you aren't interested in society and culture, there's no reason to read it. You may love to bicycle and therefore bicycles.misc"; other people might find pedestrian (pun intended).

How ... are the topics in Usenet news? Some examples whose names speak for themselves include

- talk.politics.guns

- alt.pets.chia

- rec.sport.baseball.data

- comp.sys.mac.portables

Usenet news is one of the most popular features of the Internet around the world. This is partially due to its wide-ranging discussions, partially due to the fact that it works almost as well with character-based clients as with graphical ones. Because it is so popular, people from all walks of life use Usenet.

As one of the oldest Internet services, Usenet has spawned the greatest number of client programs. Some of these are quite advanced, letting you browse through hundreds of messages very quickly. These programs allow you to organize the messages by topic name, so that you can ignore whole groups of messages on

client programs
Software that interfaces with server programs. A client program often looks different on each computer that runs it, taking on each computer's best features. Many different client programs can interact with one server program.

subjects that don't interest you. The programs also let you easily compose replies to messages. A few Web clients, notably Netscape, have Usenet clients built into them.

Which brings up one side of Usenet that you might not find so pleasant. In Usenet news, some people have a tendency to be rude and crude. (Or, to be polite about it, these individuals are "socially challenged.") This is to say they probably think and act that way in their regular lives as well, but you may not want to be around them when they do.

Sometimes these people show up in newsgroups where the discussion is usually quite nice. On the other hand, there are entire groups for this kind of discussion. (If you really want to see, one such group is "alt.tasteless.") And, just as one's person's fun is another person's horror, there are lots of *alt.* groups (and some *rec.* and *sci.* and *talk.* groups) that you may find quite offensive.

Many newsgroups have discussions that are incredibly informative and often don't seem like they are on a computer network. For some people, these newsgroups may serve as their major contact for discussing important issues; for other people, it's just a good way to chat with hundreds of people about nontechnical things they like.

A small sampling of such groups includes

- **talk.rape** Often includes postings from rape survivors and people working to reduce the incidence of rape

- **rec.pets.cats** Everything from cat psychology to how to eliminate fleas

- **soc.culture.indian** A wide-ranging discussion that includes people in India and many, often homesick, expatriates

- **k12.chat.junior** Discussions among folks in grades 6-8 or so

- **misc.handicap** Disabilities of many types

Mailing Lists

In the early days of the Internet, before Usenet newsgroups were common, the most interesting discussions happened on mailing lists. A mailing list is a way of sending copies of a single letter to a large group of people all at once. Some mailing lists are only five or ten people; others have more than 500 people on them.

mailing list A list of users who receive copies of mail messages. When a user sends a message to the mailing list, all users on the list receive a copy. Some mailing lists reach thousands of people.

Unless you use a very advanced mail client program, getting information from mailing lists is definitely more difficult than getting information from Usenet newsgroups. Because all your mail comes to one box, if you are on two or three mailing lists, it is difficult to separate which messages are from which list. With Usenet, you always know which newsgroup you are looking at.

Because Usenet news generally has a better interface, not as much effort has been put into mailing lists in the past few years. Even so, there are still thousands of active mailing lists that cover a wide variety of topics. Generally, a mailing list on a particular topic is read by far fewer people than the number of people reading from a Usenet newsgroup on the same topic.

Mailing List Features

This is not to imply that mailing lists are no good. In fact, they have many advantages over Usenet news. Some major features of mailing lists that can't be matched by Usenet news include

▶ You don't have to be able to run Usenet to read mailing lists. Although more and more Internet users have access to Usenet, not everyone can (or wants) to read Usenet newsgroups. Even among those who do, some people are too timid to go beyond using mail.

LISTSERV A program that manages mailing lists. LISTSERV has an arcane interface, but has been around for over a decade. Computers running LISTSERV still manage many important mailing lists. You can send commands to many LISTSERV mailing lists to retrieve files.

▶ You don't need to get permission from others on the Internet to set up a mailing list. You probably do need the permission (and help) of your system administrator, but that is usually easy to get. If you want to discuss a very small topic, and you don't think tens of thousands of people are interested, setting up a mailing list can take only a few minutes, if you are given proper assistance at your Internet site.

▶ Many mailing lists tend to be more focused than their Usenet counterparts. For example, you may be interested in the treatment of a particular kind of cancer. The Usenet newsgroups about cancer discuss all kinds of cancer, and all aspects of cancer, not just treatment. A mailing list that is specifically about the topic you are interested in may not get much traffic, but it will most likely be of more value to you.

▶ Mailing lists can be private. The mailing list administrator can choose who to let on the list. This can be used to limit the discussion to experts, or to exclude people who are abusive, or to force people who read the group to also post interesting information.

Finding Lists

There are a few listings of mailing lists, but no definitive central repository, so you need to conduct a thorough search before you give up on your quest. The most common list is the "Publicly Accessible Mailing Lists" (PAML) list that appears periodically in the Usenet "news.answers" newsgroup. That document (which is quite large and comes in many parts) lists hundreds of mailing lists, their descriptions, and how to join them.

Sample Lists

The following paragraphs are a few samples from the PAML list that relate to music. There are thousands of other mailing lists such as these.

Elvis Costello

Contact: costello-request@gnu.ai.mit.edu
(Danny Hernandez)

Purpose: For the discussion and dissemination of information about Declan Patrick Aloysius MacManus, better known as Elvis Costello. Everyone is welcome.

folk_music

Contact: listserv@nysernet.org (Alan Rowoth)
Purpose: Folk_music is a moderated discussion list dealing with the music of the recent wave of American singer/songwriters. List traffic consists of tour schedules, reviews, album release information, and other information on artists such as Shawn Colvin, Mary-Chapin Carpenter, David Wilcox, Nanci Griffith, Darden Smith, Cheryl Wheeler, John Gorka, Ani DiFranco, and others. There are no archives as of yet.

To subscribe, send mail to <listserv@nysernet.org> with this request: SUBSCRIBE FOLK_MUSIC Your Fullname

Network-Audio-Bits

Contact: Murph@Maine.BITNET (Michael A. Murphy)

Purpose: Network Audio Bits & Audio Software Review is a bi-monthly electronic magazine that features reviews of and information about current rock, pop, New Age, jazz, funk, folk, and other musical genres. A mixture of major label artists and independent recording artists can be found reviewed in these "pages."

Mailing List Netiquette

As is usual on the Internet, particular rules govern how to join and leave mailing lists. Although different lists have different rules, one rule of netiquette is almost universal: don't send mail directly to the list to join. Almost every list has a second mailing address that is used for administration such as subscribing, getting files, and so on. The hundreds of people on the list don't want to see your request to get on the list itself.

Once you are on a mailing list, remember that anything you send to the list is sent to everyone. If someone asks a specific question, send a reply to just them at their mail address, don't send it to the whole list (unless you are pretty sure that it is a universal problem for which you have a very good solution).

The best thing to do as you get started in the world of mailing lists is not to say anything for about a week after you join. Get the feel for the conversation. Note how busy or not busy the list is. Notice how others get treated when they commit typical beginner's blunders. See if there are other things you should be doing at the same time (such as reading Usenet newsgroups). And remember that everyone on the list is a human who wants to be treated the way you want to be treated.

Anonymous FTP

An Internet relic that remains popular to this day is *FTP*, an acronym for the less-than-enticingly named *file transfer protocol*. You have probably guessed what FTP does: lets you transfer files to and from Internet hosts. Although services such as the World Wide Web and Gopher do this as well as FTP and have much nicer interfaces, FTP is still widely used and is one of the best ways to get shareware and freeware for your personal computer.

When you attach to another computer through FTP, you can navigate through its disk directories like you can on your own computer. The directories often have names that indicate their contents, although the names are much shorter and less descriptive than you might hope. Most FTP servers run on UNIX systems, and the filenames on some systems reflect that (for better or worse).

Downloading Files

When you find a file or group of files that you want to download, you copy them to your host computer. From there, you can copy them to your personal computer. If you connect to the Internet through a SLIP or PPP connection, you can FTP files directly to your personal computer's hard disk.

Almost all FTP host computers will let anyone download files. This type of FTP is called *anonymous FTP* because

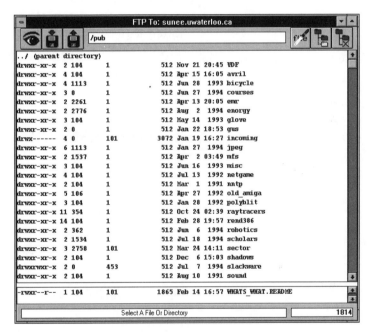

▶ *Thousands of FTP servers have hundreds of thousands of files to download. This shows just some of the categories on one server, at the University of Waterloo in Ontario, Canada. As with many FTP sites, files about academics, recreation, programming, and so on are available.*

download Using data communication links to copy a file from a remote system to your computer. Downloading files from anonymous FTP servers is a popular way to get freeware and shareware files.

Archie A program that lets you search a list of files that you can download from other host computers using anonymous FTP.

everyone logs into the FTP host using the same user name. On many systems, it is not truly anonymous, however, because you must provide your e-mail address before you can download files.

As with other Internet services, the range of things you can find through anonymous FTP is amazing. There are hosts with pictures, books, magazines, and so on. All the best shareware and freeware for the PC and Macintosh is available by anonymous FTP from dozens of sites on the Internet. Even though there are far fewer Macintoshes than PCs, almost as many interesting Macintosh programs are available by FTP. Huge collections of computer-related manuals and instructional guides are also available by anonymous FTP.

▶ When you log into most FTP sites, they give you information about the site and where to find the most popular files. Usually, there are also files with names such as "README" that give you more information.

```
drwx------     2 0          0           1024 Sep 20 02:59 .admin
-rw-r--r--     1 0          1         255390 Sep 20 02:58 INDEX
-r--r--r--     1 0          1         108939 Sep 20 02:59 INDEX.ZIP
-r--r--r--     1 0          1          65406 Sep 20 03:00 LS-LTR.ZIP
-r--r--r--     1 0          0           1162 Mar 24  1994 MIRROR_SITE_INFO
-r--r--r--     1 0          0          17052 Aug 18 15:03 README
drwxr-xr-x     2 0          0           1024 Sep 13 04:15 access
drwxr-xr-x     2 0          0           3584 Sep 20 02:55 demo
drwxr-xr-x     2 0          0          13312 Sep 20 02:58 desktop
-r--r--r--     1 0          0            496 Dec  5  1993 dirtree
drwxr-xr-x     4 0          0            512 Aug 17  1993 drivers
drwxr-xr-x     2 0          0            512 Aug 16 03:31 excel
drwxr-xr-x     4 0          0           2560 Sep 20 02:50 fonts
drwxr-xr-x     2 0          0           6656 Sep 20 02:50 games
drwxr-xr-x     2 0          0           1536 Sep  1 22:43 icons
-r--r--r--     1 0          0           7195 Sep 20 03:00 last100uploads
-rw-r--r--     1 0          1         261069 Sep 20 02:59 ls-ltR
drwxr-xr-x     2 0          0           8704 Sep 20 02:58 misc
drwxr-xr-x     2 0          0           6656 Sep 20 02:50 nt
drwxr-xr-x     2 0          0            512 Aug  9 16:26 pagemkr
drwxr-xr-x     3 0          0           1536 Aug 23 02:51 patches
drwxr-xr-x     2 0          0            512 Aug 30 13:19 pdoxwin
drwxr-xr-x     2 0          1           1536 Sep 20 04:00 pending.uploads
drwxr-xr-x     6 0          0           4096 Sep 20 02:50 programr
drwxr-xr-x     2 0          0            512 Feb 22  1994 sdl
drwxr-xr-x     2 0          0           5120 Sep 20 02:50 sounds
drwxr-xr-x     2 0          0           1536 Sep  1 22:42 toolbook
d-wx-wx-wx     2 0          1           4096 Sep 20 03:57 uploads
drwxr-xr-x     2 0          0          21504 Sep 20 02:58 util
drwxr-xr-x     2 0          0           2048 Sep 20 02:50 winsock
drwxr-xr-x     2 0          0           2048 Sep 20 02:50 winword
drwxr-xr-x     2 0          0            512 Jun  7 03:48 wpwin
drwxr-xr-x     2 0          0            512 Feb 22  1994 wrk
226 Transfer complete.
ftp>
```

▶ *A popular site for programs that relate to Microsoft Windows is the CICA (Center for Innovative Computer Application) archives at Indiana University.*

anonymous FTP The use of the FTP program to connect to a host computer on the Internet, access its public directories, and transfer files from the host computer to your computer. Anonymous FTP is the most common way to search for and download files. Hundreds of host computers on the Internet let anyone look through their file directories for files they want in this way.

```
Connected to gowinnt.microsoft.com.
220 ftp Windows NT FTP Server (Version 3.5).
Name (ftp.microsoft.com:phoffman): anonymous
331 Anonymous access allowed, send identity (e-mail name) as password.
Password:
230-!
  | Welcome to ftp.microsoft.com (a.k.a gowinnt.microsoft.com)!
  |
  | Please enter your "full e-mail name" as your password.
  |     Report any problems to ftp@microsoft.com
  |
  | Refer to the index.txt file for further information
  |
230 Anonymous user logged in as anonymous.
Remote system type is Windows_NT.
ftp> dir
200 PORT command successful.
150 Opening ASCII mode data connection for /bin/ls.
dr-xr-xr-x   1 owner    group              0 Aug 23 16:23 advsys
dr-xr-xr-x   1 owner    group              0 Aug 24  5:37 deskapps
dr-xr-xr-x   1 owner    group              0 Aug 24 10:52 developr
-r-xr-xr-x   1 owner    group           4161 Sep 19  7:43 dirmap.txt
-r-xr-xr-x   1 owner    group            712 Aug 25 15:07 disclaimer.txt
-r-xr-xr-x   1 owner    group            860 Sep  1  8:40 index.txt
-r-xr-xr-x   1 owner    group         521870 Sep 19  0:22 LS-LR.ZIP
dr-xr-xr-x   1 owner    group              0 Aug 24 12:36 MSEdCert
dr-xr-xr-x   1 owner    group              0 Aug 22 16:24 MSFT
-r-xr-xr-x   1 owner    group          28160 Nov 29  1993 MSNBRO.DOC
-r-xr-xr-x   1 owner    group          22641 Feb  8  9:58 MSNBRO.TXT
-r-xr-xr-x   1 owner    group              0 Aug 24 15:09 peropsys
dr-xr-xr-x   1 owner    group              0 Sep  9 11:23 Softlib
-r-xr-xr-x   1 owner    group           5095 Oct 20  1993 support-phone#.txt
dr-xr-xr-x   1 owner    group              0 Aug 22 16:38 TechNet
-r-xr-xr-x   1 owner    group            802 Aug 25  8:09 WhatHappened.txt
226 Transfer complete.
ftp>
```

▶ *Many commercial companies also have FTP sites. Microsoft runs one of the largest, and busiest, FTP sites.*

Uploading Files

Some Internet sites also let you upload files to their anonymous FTP servers, meaning you can make new material available to those servers. For example, if you have written a program you want others to be able to access, you can send it by FTP to some of the popular anonymous FTP sites. Many of the sites duplicate each other, so your file may quickly propagate throughout the Internet. Of course, for every person who contributes files, there are thousands who just download files. But if you want others to see what you have done, distribution through FTP is easy and costs you nothing.

FTP Client Software

Most of the client software for FTP is not nearly as easy to use as client software for other Internet services. Only a few graphical FTP clients exist, and they don't offer much more than the character-based clients. However, that situation is beginning to change because Web browsers such as Mosaic and Netscape also allow access to FTP servers. Because FTP will probably be popular for many years, these Web clients are starting to add features that will make using FTP easier, such as automatically showing messages when you enter an FTP directory.

```
-rw-r--r--   1 macmod   other       1987 May  3 15:28 00readme.txt
lrwxrwxrwx   1 macmod   other          3 May 12 18:38 AntiVirus -> vir
lrwxrwxrwx   1 macmod   other          3 May 12 18:38 Application -> app
lrwxrwxrwx   1 macmod   other          4 May 12 18:39 Communication -> comm
lrwxrwxrwx   1 macmod   other          3 May 12 18:39 Compress-Translate -> cmp
lrwxrwxrwx   1 macmod   other          3 May 12 18:39 Configuration -> cfg
lrwxrwxrwx   1 macmod   other          3 May 12 18:42 Development -> dev
lrwxrwxrwx   1 macmod   other          4 May 12 18:42 Disk-File -> disk
lrwxrwxrwx   1 macmod   other          4 May 12 18:42 Font -> font
lrwxrwxrwx   1 macmod   other          4 May 12 18:43 Game -> game
lrwxrwxrwx   1 macmod   other          3 Jun  6 13:43 Graphic -> grf
lrwxrwxrwx   1 macmod   other          4 May 12 18:43 Help -> help
lrwxrwxrwx   1 macmod   other          4 May 12 18:44 Hypercard -> card
lrwxrwxrwx   1 macmod   other          4 May 12 18:44 Information -> info
lrwxrwxrwx   1 macmod   other          3 May 12 18:44 Newton -> nwt
lrwxrwxrwx   1 macmod   other          3 May 12 18:44 Periodical -> per
lrwxrwxrwx   1 macmod   other          3 May 12 18:45 Print -> prn
lrwxrwxrwx   1 macmod   other          3 May 12 18:45 Recent -> rec
lrwxrwxrwx   1 macmod   other          3 May 12 18:45 Science-Math -> sci
lrwxrwxrwx   1 macmod   other          3 May 12 18:45 Sound -> snd
lrwxrwxrwx   1 macmod   other          4 May 12 18:45 TextProcessing -> text
lrwxrwxrwx   1 macmod   other          3 May 12 18:45 UserInterface -> gui
lrwxrwxrwx   1 macmod   other          4 Jun 19 04:18 Utility -> util
```

▶ *The preeminent FTP site for Macintosh programs and files is Info-Mac at Stanford University.*

Mail Response Systems

Not everyone on the Internet has access to anonymous FTP. In fact, most people don't. However, that doesn't mean that those people cannot get files from Internet hosts. Some hosts have a service that lets you request files by mail. The service then returns the requested file to your electronic mailbox.

These mail response systems have many purposes. For example, if your company wants Internet users to be able to get information about your product or services, a mail response system is probably the best way to distribute literature to the widest possible Internet audience. Even if you have dozens of different files you want to make available, it is fairly easy to explain to mail users how to request the specific files.

FTP File transfer protocol, the Internet's file transfer program. FTP is one of the older standards on the Internet, and most FTP client software is fairly unfriendly and difficult to use. On the other hand, FTP is still an efficient way to transfer files between systems and to distribute information on request to Internet users.

Interacting with Mail Response Systems

There is no standard method for interacting with mail response systems — there isn't even a standard name for them. Some people call them "file mailers," others call them "files-by-mail," and so on. Generally, if you send a message to the correct mail address for the mail response system, even if you don't word your message at all correctly, you will get a reply telling you how to use the system to get the files you want.

Most mail response systems deliver files only from that one service. Some systems, however, will send you any file that is available by anonymous FTP. While these systems can be a boon for Internet users without anonymous FTP access, they are usually terribly slow, often taking anywhere from a day to a week to return the file. Thus, you probably want to use them only as a last resort.

host On the Internet and other networks, a host is the computer that performs centralized functions. For example, a host makes program or data files available to computers on the Internet.

Getting Basic Information

No central list of all the mail response systems on the Internet is available. If you think that a particular host computer might have such a system, you are usually safe in sending a message to "info" at that system, such as "info@suntree.com." The "info" user has become a sort of Internet standard for the place to ask for information about the system. Note, however, the "info" mailbox is sometimes answered by a human, so you might consider asking for help in the same manner you would on the telephone.

Using most mail response systems is pretty easy. Most systems require you to put a one-line command in the message of your mail such as "send price-list" or "mail EntryForm." Others are a bit more arcane, forcing you to know a bit more about UNIX's file system and so on. However, you can generally get the hang of a particular mail response system in one or two tries.

Library Catalogs Through Telnet

Another venerable Internet service that doesn't seem to die is *telnet*, which is a simple way to give you a connection on another host. Using telnet is like using a terminal program on your personal computer to connect to a remote computer. All that telnet does is let your computer behave as though it's a simple terminal on the remote computer.

These days, few Internet sites allow you to use telnet to connect to them, for both interface and security reasons. Two types of services do, however, still offer connections through telnet: library catalogs and bulletin board systems.

Accessing Library Catalogs

Many libraries invested a great deal of money on their catalog software in the 1980s, and thus don't want to spend any more money to change the interface. Hundreds of college and public libraries allow anyone on the Internet to access their catalogs, even though only a tiny number of those people can actually borrow books from those libraries. There is even a centralized list of all such libraries, called Hytelnet, which helps you find the library closest to you.

Connecting to Bulletin Board Systems

Most bulletin board systems (BBSs) allow people to dial them only directly. However, more and more BBSs are beginning to recognize the importance of the Internet as a communications medium and have started to allow people to connect to them over telnet. By allowing telnet access, these BBSs let people from all over the world become members as long as they have local Internet access.

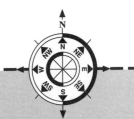

telnet An Internet service that lets one computer act as a terminal on another computer. Using telnet, you can type on another computer as if you were directly connected to it. In this way, telnet is like common communications programs (sometimes called "terminal programs") for personal computers.

Hytelnet A program that works with telnet to let you easily browse through library catalogs. Hytelnet has a database of all known public library catalogs and information about how to operate them when you are connected to them.

However, telnet is rapidly falling out of style for Internet services. Telnet uses up a fair amount of the host computer's resources and generally presents you with a rather unattractive user interface after you reach the remote host. It is only a matter of time until library catalogs switch again, this time probably to the World Wide Web, which is incredibly well suited to large catalogs. In the next ten years, many bulletin boards will probably switch from their plain character interfaces and telnet to the World Wide Web, because its interface is much more attractive to individual users.

MUD A program that simulates a place where you can move around, talk to other users, and interact with your surroundings. MUD stands for Multi-User Dimensions (or Multi-User Dungeons), and most are centered around fantasy themes such as dragons and science fiction. Many Internet MUDs even let you create parts of the environment for others to use.

Multi-User Dimensions

In the late 1970s, as the Internet was just getting off the ground, many early PC owners became captivated by role-playing games, the most popular of which was *Zork*. These games involve fantasy themes in which you roam around a large environment while gaining treasure and killing beasts. These games are still popular, but have evolved greatly.

What Are MUDs?

These early fantasy games were fun, but they were designed for a single person. Internet users came up with a way to allow many users to interact in these fantasy worlds, with each user having their own character, their own powers, and so on. The worlds are called *Multi-User Dimensions* or *Multi-User Dungeons* — MUD for short.

You connect to MUDs through telnet. Hundreds of MUDs are available, and more appear every week. Some MUDs allow you to play only the game designed by the MUD wizard; others let you (if you can program) extend the environment of the MUD by creating new monsters, new areas to explore, new weapons, and so on.

Needless to say, some people are quite entranced by MUDs. It can be particularly fun to play on some active MUDs when different Internet users join forces. Some MUDs have very little action and are mostly for discussion. However, even on these MUDs, people often take on fantasy personae.

Sample MUD

This is part of what you might see on an adventure MUD. The parts in boldface are what were typed by the user; everything else is displayed by the MUD computer.

You have now entered a huge tavern that seems abandoned. On the walls are many elaborate tapestries that seem almost too-vividly colored. You hear a low hum.

north

You are at the north end of the deserted tavern. The hum has grown louder, and it is now accompanied by a distinct rustle. But there is no wind. There is a window here, covered with years of grime.

open window

The window creeeeeks open. You can see a meadow of mostly dry grass. Suddenly one of the tapestries bursts into flame and the figures from the tapestry come alive. Unfortunately, this was a tapestry picturing three grotesque magars, and these now-embodied beings are coming at you with their wyliak clubs drawn menacingly.

north

You try to climb out the window, but you get stuck. Maybe you should have measured it first, because it is clearly narrower than your hips. The magars are now closer.

use dagger

Violence again, eh? You wave the dagger in front of you, as if to scare off the magars. Two of them take you seriously; one doesn't.

thrust dagger

Even though your energy is low, you still have good aim. You give a deep nick to the magar's good arm, causing him to shriek loudly.

The magars all run toward the flaming tapestry, leap onto it, and it suddenly stops burning. The magars in the picture glare at you. One of them holds his good arm with both his other arms, and you see a bit of fresh blood on the tapestry where you nicked the magar.

west

You leave the main room of the tavern, entering a dark side-chamber that smells somewhat of old chocolate and wet dogs. There is a strange fire here.

look fire

This is a small, portable fire shaped like a two hearts. It sings many beautiful songs that can help you in many difficult situations. It burns the incense of the soul.

take fire

You pick up the fire and it moves directly to your heart. Your power level has increased to 8.3.

east

You are at the north end of the deserted tavern. There is a very loud hum and a rustle that sounds like the wings of dray-bats.

▶ *As people play MUDs, they often imagine the scene that goes with the text they are reading on-screen.*

Chat and IRC

For most people, the telephone is a great form of communication. Pick it up, dial a seven- or ten-digit number, and you can talk to the person you want (or, more likely, their answering machine). Conversing on the telephone isn't perfect, though. Long-distance telephone calls are not cheap, especially if you call another country.

chat An old Internet multiuser discussion system. It has almost completely been replaced by Internet Relay Chat (IRC).

Also, the telephone is only the best solution if you know with whom you want to speak. Some people are just in the mood to talk with anyone, a stranger or a vague acquaintance. To many people, this may not sound very appealing, but to others it's just the right balance of intimacy and distance.

Chatting on the Internet

Although it often seems quite limiting, many people like to chat over the Internet. With the *chat* and *IRC* (Internet Relay Chat) programs, you can connect to anyone else on the Internet who is also chatting and, well, chat. The interface isn't elaborate: you type lines and they type lines. Some people prefer chat to mail, however, because it is immediate.

Liking to use the Internet for chatting with other folks is an acquired taste. For some people, IRC is lots of fun and easy. For others, it is incredibly difficult to use because conversations are disjointed. For example, a conversation might go as follows:

(Morgan): Where did you find that, Ruth?

(John): I can't believe you spent that much time looking for a new futon!

(Ruth): At Timberwolf Guitars. Where did you get yours?

(Zoriah): I bought my first guitar there!

Internet Relay Chat (IRC) A program that lets many people talk at the same time by typing. Using IRC is similar to being in many conversations at once at a party.

(Tessa): Futons are pretty expensive around here. I miss living in a city.

(Morgan): Where?

(John): Oh, okay. I forgot where you live.

(Ruth): To whom were you talking, Zoriah?

(Zoriah): Ruth, where do you live?

(Zoriah): To Ruth.

(John): It's late, gotta go. 'Nite all!

(Ruth): Zoriah, I live up in Maine. Where do you live?

(John): Sleep well, y'all!

(Tessa): Night, John! So, Z, did you pass that test you were moaning about?

(Zoriah): In Vermont. And, yes Tessa, I did. Got an A, actually.

You get the idea. You get lots of cross-talk, lots of confusion, and so on. For some people, this is just fine. For others, it will drive them crazy faster than anything. You might or might not find IRC interesting.

Finding the Right Channel

IRC is like chatting at a well-organized party. Different discussions are going on in many places, and the names of the discussions often tell you the theme. The discussion names, called "channels," exist even when no one is currently talking in them. At any given time you might find discussions on

▶ Sports, often about specific teams

▶ Local politics in many areas

- Sex (always a popular topic, it seems)

- Various computer games and how to beat them

- Jobs and companies to work for

There are many graphical IRC clients available. These clients let you monitor and interact with many different channels, and have a different window open for each channel. You can use this feature to monitor five or more lightly used channels while you do your other work or, if you are good at juggling conversations, to participate in many conversations at once.

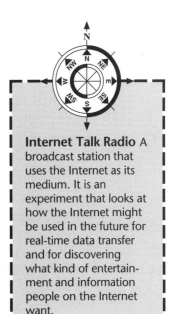

Internet Talk Radio A broadcast station that uses the Internet as its medium. It is an experiment that looks at how the Internet might be used in the future for real-time data transfer and for discovering what kind of entertainment and information people on the Internet want.

Internet Talk Radio

The Internet is a great distribution medium for many kinds of information. As you have already seen, person-to-person services — mail, group discussions on Usenet, and so on — are available on the Internet. Another service that has appeared recently gives a glimpse of the Internet's future: Internet Talk Radio.

At first, the idea of a radio show over the Internet may seem like a waste of resources, but one of the many purposes of Internet Talk Radio is to determine alternative and interesting ways to distribute information over the Internet. Not everyone likes to read news in mail or Usenet: they'd rather listen to it.

Internet Talk Radio is modeled after National Public Radio: it has sponsors (not advertisers), covers a wide range of topics, and the target audience consists of people who care about the Internet. The weekly half-hour show is quite large, about 15 megabytes, so it is most appropriate for people who have high-speed direct connections to the Internet.

Accessing Internet Talk Radio

Because the weekly files are so large, Internet Talk Radio is distributed — instead of downloaded — to reduce Internet traffic. Dozens of companies get the file and make it available on their local networks so that many people at the site don't waste time downloading it from the Internet individually. There are also many servers throughout the world to make it easier to get it from a local location.

Internet Talk Radio also points out some of the weaknesses of the Internet as it stands today. Not everyone can play sound on their computers, so those people cannot receive Internet Talk Radio. Also, no single standard has been set for how sound should be played. Even if everyone could play sound in the same manner on their computers, 15 megabytes is an unreasonable amount of data for people to download via modem.

The content of Internet Talk Radio isn't for everyone. It is often very technical, with many discussions about how to support the future growth of the Internet. However, it is an interesting experiment in what the Internet might offer in the short term and in how to sensibly distribute large files.

Finger

Internet users have found incredibly creative ways for distributing information in oddball fashions. Most of the distribution methods discussed so far have to be set up by a system administrator. At some sites, however, the system administrator is too busy or just plain uninterested in helping end users provide information to other Internet users.

Using the Finger Program

In the past few years, more and more people have used the *finger program* as a mechanism for publishing. The finger program is a UNIX command that is normally used to tell someone else if you are logged on and if you are not, how long it's been since you were. Some versions of the finger program also let you include information about yourself as a way to let others learn a bit about you without having to send mail to you.

This second feature has spawned a "small cottage industry" in people putting interesting things in their finger information. For instance, some people include a joke of the day, sports scores, astronomical data, strange statistics, and so on. Anyone who has a finger

finger An Internet service that tells you information about a user on another computer, such as when the user last logged on. Not all computers run finger servers.

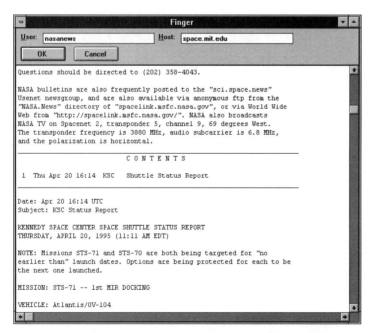

▶ *The latest news from NASA can be obtained from MIT by using finger on the address "nasanews@space.mit.edu."*

UNIX A computer operating system originally developed by AT&T Bell Laboratories. UNIX is the most common operating system for servers and hosts on the Internet. Almost any computer can be an Internet host, but computers running UNIX are historically the most common Internet hosts.

client (which is most people with UNIX connections to the Internet) can see the information by using the mail address of the desired account.

However, many Internet sites do not support users publishing information through the finger program. For security reasons, they deny all finger requests to their systems. Some sites just reject the requests without explanation; others give a message such as the following:

Thank you for requesting information from our host computer. However, we do not support the "finger" command for any users. The user whom you asked about may or may not exist on the system: this message is generated for all requests regardless of whether or not the user actually exists.

▶ For the latest sports schedules, birthdays, and special days, you can try "copi@oddjob.uchicago.edu."

WAIS Databases

Searching through millions of Internet files for just the piece of information you want is an impossible task. Thousands of host computers are connected to the Internet, and given the lack of central structure to the Internet, there is no single location where you can look for everything.

All is not lost, however. Many Internet hosts have adopted a standard called *WAIS* (Wide Area Information Server) that lets sites create databases that can be accessed on the Internet. The underlying part of WAIS uses a standard type of query (called Z39.50); however, WAIS client software shields you from having to know anything about it by letting you ask for information in almost plain English.

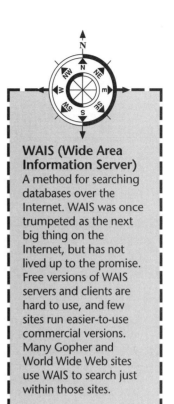

WAIS (Wide Area Information Server)
A method for searching databases over the Internet. WAIS was once trumpeted as the next big thing on the Internet, but has not lived up to the promise. Free versions of WAIS servers and clients are hard to use, and few sites run easier-to-use commercial versions. Many Gopher and World Wide Web sites use WAIS to search just within those sites.

WAIS Features

When you start searching WAIS for information, you first specify which databases you want to search. You can search in many databases at once, which is one feature that makes WAIS different from most databases available. Of course, if you list too many databases for your search, your search can take quite a long time.

Another advanced feature of WAIS is that it uses *relevance feedback*, which is a fancy way of

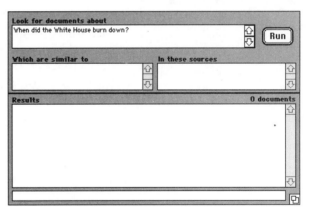

▶ *With many WAIS clients, you can make your queries much like English.*

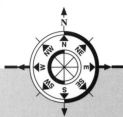

client/server software
Software that is split between a server, which performs most underlying processing, and a client, which mostly communicates with the user. The term client/server has become widely used in the computer industry to describe database and information retrieval systems where the user runs a program on a personal computer that interacts with a database program on a host computer. Most of the major Internet services (such as mail, Usenet news, and the World Wide Web) use the client/server model.

saying that you can modify your requests based on what you find. For example, assume that you are searching for information about the city of Houston. Your request might come back with lots of information you aren't interested in. You can create a new search indicating you want to see only information that is somewhat like the information you received and considered to be useful responses.

The Future of WAIS

When it was introduced a few years ago, WAIS seemed like a panacea for distributing information from databases. However, interest in WAIS has lagged due to the lack of support for the free WAIS tools that were initially developed. (There are also commercial implementations of WAIS.) Also, WAIS clients are not as easy to use as Gopher and Web clients. Some sites do have very good luck distributing data through WAIS, but it is mostly used as a local search engine in those instances.

This last use may keep interest in WAIS alive. Many Web and Gopher server software packages have built-in connections to WAIS, so people who are putting up Web servers have an incentive to use WAIS instead of building in different connections. However, other good database programs that can be hooked into Web and Gopher servers are available. Internet users like the ability to search through databases, but they don't demand it. Like other Internet tools, WAIS will flourish or founder based on myriad free market pressures.

PART 4

Where to Go and What to Do on the Internet

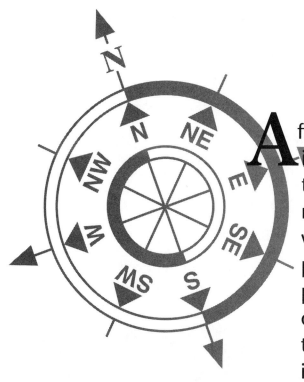

After you know how to get the information you want from the Internet, you're ready to roll. The Internet has such a wide variety of things to read, people to meet, and groups to participate in, that you may be overwhelmed. This section tells you what kind of fascinating things you can find in the nooks and crannies of the Internet.

Weather

No matter where you are in the world, people are concerned about the weather and like to talk about it. Talk about politics and religion may rise and fall, but folks are always interested in what the weather is like today, what the weather will be like tomorrow, and wasn't the weather awful last winter. Because of this level of interest, the Internet has many areas and host computers devoted to weather.

Usenet A widely used Internet service that organizes people's comments by topic. These topics, called newsgroups, have their own structure, with people commenting on previous comments and starting new discussions. Usenet is the second most popular Internet feature, after mail.

World Wide Web (WWW) An Internet service that lets users retrieve hypertext and graphics from various sites. Often called just "the Web," the World Wide Web has become one of the most popular Internet services in the past two years. In fact, many Internet information providers publish using only the Web.

Usenet newsgroups in many areas around the world discuss their local weather. Here is a partial list of the group "ba.weather" that discusses the weather in the San Francisco Bay Area.

▶ Redding Area Daily Climatological Report

▶ Reno Area Daily Climatological Report

▶ Sacramento Area Daily Climatological Report

▶ California weather summary

▶ Ultraviolet light forecast

Many of the postings are automatically generated and others are discussions among humans.

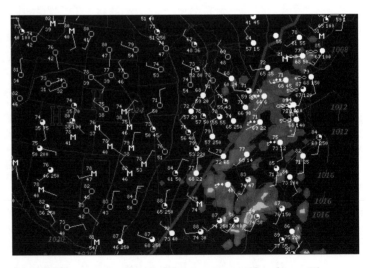

▶ At MIT, you can check the current weather by getting a map of the United States through the World Wide Web. The map looks quite busy, but you can find out about specific areas just by clicking on the map.

The National Oceanic and Atmospheric Administration (NOAA) collects environmental information from 10,000 locations around the world. You can obtain information about current weather conditions at practically any location, and get oceanographic data as well, from the NOAA Gopher site. Some weather servers also have information about environmental changes that are happening around the world.

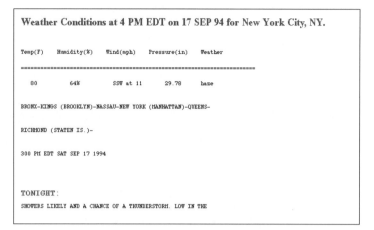

▶ *For example, clicking on New York gives you this type of data.*

▶ *Some Internet sites also keep pictures from historical weather systems, such as Hurricane Andrew.*

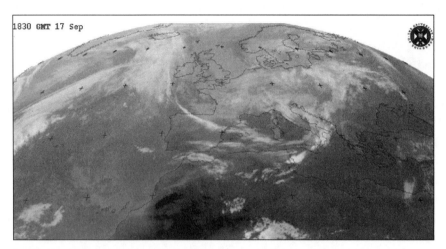

1830 GMT 17 Sep

▶ Of course, you might be interested in weather outside the United States, and there are plenty of sites around the world with maps and data for their locations.

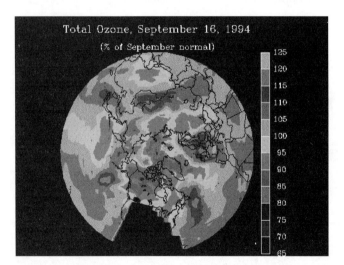

Total Ozone, September 16, 1994
(% of September normal)

▶ Global warming and the size of the ozone hole have been of concern to many people. You can download historical information and current ozone concentration charts from many Internet sites.

Downloadable Files

One of the most popular features of bulletin board systems (BBSs) is the files that you can download. Various hosts on the Internet also have files that you can download. In fact, the most popular files on the largest systems, such as CompuServe and America Online, are almost always available on the Internet within a day or two of them appearing elsewhere; some appear on the Internet first.

Some files are of interest only to people with particular computers. If you have a PC, you probably aren't interested in programs that run only on the Macintosh. However, many files are of interest to people regardless of the brand of their computer. Most

```
ftp> dir
200 PORT command successful.
150 Opening ASCII mode data connection for /bin/ls.
total 218
drwxr-xr-x    6 5715   5715      512 Apr 10 23:41 CIS
-rw-r--r--    1 5715   5715     8950 Aug  9 16:16 CW-danceplaces.txt
drwxr-xr-x    2 5715   5715     1536 Sep 11 16:03 CW-dancesteps
-rw-r--r--    1 5715   5715     5071 May 18 01:28 IDSF-orgs.txt
drwxr-xr-x    4 5715   5715      512 Sep  8 01:09 NA
drwxr-xr-x    5 5715   5715      512 Jun  5 20:04 UK
-rw-r--r--    1 5715   5715     3360 Jul  2 19:20 WRRC-orgs.txt
drwxr-xr-x    4 5715   5715      512 Apr  9 05:58 africa
drwxr-xr-x   14 5715   5715      512 Apr  9 06:05 asia
drwxr-xr-x    2 5715   5715      512 Sep 10 23:41 ballroom-contacts
drwxr-xr-x    2 5715   5715      512 Feb 11  1994 bermuda
drwxr-xr-x    2 5715   5715      512 Jul  8 22:16 books
drwxr-xr-x    2 5715   5715      512 Feb 11  1994 brazil
drwxr-xr-x    2 5715   5715      512 Feb 11  1994 clip-art
drwxr-xr-x    2 5715   5715      512 Feb 11  1994 dominican-republic
drwxr-xr-x   23 5715   5715      512 Aug 30 00:46 europa
drwxr-xr-x    2 5715   5715      512 Sep 10 23:41 folk-dancing
drwxr-xr-x    2 5715   5715      512 Jul  3 05:23 ireland-UK-topics
drwxr-xr-x    2 5715   5715      512 Feb 11  1994 israel
drwxr-xr-x    2 5715   5715      512 Jun  5 17:19 magazines
-rw-r--r--    1 5715   5715     3582 Feb  5  1994 mailorder.txt
drwxr-xr-x    2 5715   5715      512 Aug  1 04:01 music
-rw-r--r--    1 5715   5715    20099 Aug 22 14:39 organizations.txt
drwxr-xr-x    2 5715   5715      512 Jun  6 00:03 other-resources
-rw-r--r--    1 5715   5715    11264 Jan  4  1980 quest.doc
-rw-r--r--    1 5715   5715     3987 Jul 20 00:57 questnr.txt
-rw-r--r--    1 5715   5715    13632 Sep  7  1993 readme.txt
drwxr-xr-x    2 5715   5715     1024 Feb 11  1994 rec-arts-dance
-rw-r--r--    1 5715   5715    10775 Jul  5 03:41 shoes.txt
drwxr-xr-x    2 5715   5715      512 Jul 16 02:52 swing
drwxr-xr-x    2 5715   5715      512 Feb 11  1994 tango
drwxr-xr-x    2 5715   5715     1024 Aug 29 00:04 topics
drwxr-xr-x    2 5715   5715      512 Feb 11  1994 venezuela
drwxr-xr-x    2 5715   5715      512 Aug 31 05:32 videos
drwxr-xr-x    2 5715   5715      512 Feb 11  1994 youth-program
226 Transfer complete.
ftp>
```

▶ *This directory lists the size of a file, which is information that may help you decide whether you want to download it.*

bulletin board systems (BBSs) Computers that people can access through modems to use the BBSs' services. Some BBSs are on the Internet, although most are not. BBSs often have downloadable files, discussion areas, and other features that make them popular. You can use some BBSs for free, but others charge a monthly or hourly fee.

freeware Software that you can use and copy with no obligation. People write freeware because it makes them feel good or hones their programming and design skills. You are not allowed to sell or alter most freeware programs, but you can give away freeware.

host On the Internet, and other networks, a host is the computer that performs centralized functions. For example, a host makes program or data files available to computers on the Internet.

```
drwxr-xr-x    2 root     archive      8192 Sep 18 01:58 4dos
-r--r--r--    1 root     archive     11545 Sep  8 06:46 DIRLIST.TXT
-r--r--r--    1 root     archive    643167 Sep 18 23:14 FILES.IDX
-r--r--r--    1 root     archive      2967 Sep  8 12:02 README.COPYRIGHT
-r--r--r--    1 root     archive      5543 Sep 18 13:49 README.descriptions
-r--r--r--    1 root     archive     11545 Sep  8 06:46 README.dir-list
-r--r--r--    1 root     archive      9293 Sep 14 18:23 README.file-formats
-r--r--r--    1 root     archive      2701 Sep  8 11:44 README.how-to-upload
-r--r--r--    1 root     archive      2309 Sep  8 11:36 README.simtel-cdrom
-r--r--r--    1 root     archive    352545 Sep 17 17:16 SIMINDEX.ZIP
-r--r--r--    1 root     archive     43691 Aug 31 00:16 UNZIP.EXE
drwxr-xr-x    2 root     archive      8192 Sep 18 01:57 ada
drwxr-xr-x    2 root     archive      8192 Sep 18 01:57 ai
drwxr-xr-x    2 root     archive      8192 Sep 18 01:57 animate
drwxr-xr-x    2 root     archive      8192 Sep 18 01:57 archiver
drwxr-xr-x    2 root     archive      8192 Sep 18 01:57 arcutil
drwxr-xr-x    2 root     archive      8192 Sep 18 01:57 asm_mag
drwxr-xr-x    2 root     archive      8192 Sep 18 01:57 asmutil
drwxr-xr-x    2 root     archive      8192 Sep 18 01:57 astrnomy
drwxr-xr-x    2 root     archive      8192 Sep 18 01:57 at
drwxr-xr-x    2 root     archive      8192 Sep 18 01:57 autocad
drwxr-xr-x    2 root     archive      8192 Sep 18 01:57 awk
drwxr-xr-x    2 root     archive      8192 Sep 18 01:57 bakernws
drwxr-xr-x    2 root     archive      8192 Sep 18 01:57 basic
drwxr-xr-x    2 root     archive      8192 Sep 19 00:12 batutil
drwxr-xr-x    2 root     archive      8192 Sep 18 01:57 bbs
drwxr-xr-x    2 root     archive      8192 Sep 18 01:57 bbsdoor
drwxr-xr-x    2 root     archive      8192 Sep 18 01:57 bbslist
drwxr-xr-x    2 root     archive      8192 Sep 18 01:55 bible
drwxr-xr-x    2 root     archive      8192 Sep 18 01:57 binedit
drwxr-xr-x    2 root     archive      8192 Sep 18 01:57 biology
drwxr-xr-x    2 root     archive      8192 Sep 18 01:57 bootutil
drwxr-xr-x    2 root     archive      8192 Sep 18 01:57 borland
drwxr-xr-x    2 root     archive      8192 Sep 18 01:56 c
drwxr-xr-x    2 root     archive      8192 Sep 18 01:57 cad
drwxr-xr-x    2 root     archive      8192 Sep 19 00:12 calculat
drwxr-xr-x    2 root     archive      8192 Sep 18 01:57 catalog
drwxr-xr-x    2 root     archive      8192 Sep 18 01:57 cdrom
drwxr-xr-x    2 root     archive      8192 Sep 18 01:57 chemstry
drwxr-xr-x    2 root     archive      8192 Sep 18 01:56 citadel
drwxr-xr-x    2 root     archive      8192 Sep 18 01:57 clipper
```

▶ *One of the largest repositories for PC software is the Simtel PC archives. Simtel was once on a military computer, but it has now moved to a large computer at Oakland University in Rochester, Michigan.*

```
drwxr-xr-x    4 root     archive      8192 Sep  7 19:55 clarkson
drwxr-xr-x  109 root     archive      8192 Sep 19 12:13 garbo.uwasa.fi
drwxr-xr-x    2 pinard   archive      8192 Jan 19  1994 gnuish
drwxr-xr-x    4 root     archive      8192 Jan 16  1994 ka9q
lrwxrwxrwx    1 root     archive         6 May 12 05:42 msdos -> simtel
drwxr-xr-x   27 root     archive      8192 Sep 19 15:34 msdos-games
drwxr-xr-x    5 root     archive      8192 Jan 15  1994 pc-blue
drwxr-xr-x  215 root     archive      8192 Sep 19 21:53 simtel
drwxr-xr-x   10 ultrasnd archive      8192 Feb 12  1994 ultrasound
drwxr-xr-x   37 root     archive      8192 Sep 13 01:45 umich.edu
drwxr-xr-x   25 root     archive      8192 Sep 13 01:59 win3
226 Transfer complete.
ftp>
```

▶ *Another large PC site is the archive at Washington University in Saint Louis. Many of the files are the same as the Simtel archive, but many are different, so you sometimes have to check both resources to find what you want.*

picture files can be used on all types of computers (depending on the type of conversion software used), and text files can be read directly by word processors on most systems.

Most file libraries are available by anonymous FTP; some are available by Gopher and World Wide Web as well. Using the character-based FTP client software, you can get a listing of what's in each directory of a host site that has downloadable files. You then get a copy of the file using its name.

Although hundreds of sites have downloadable files, a few sites are considered the definitive host sites for the PC and for the Macintosh. Because these main sites are often very busy, they have mirrors at many other hosts around the world. Having mirrors in different countries also can reduce the traffic on the Internet because people can get the files they want from more local computers.

Not everything you get from host sites is free. A great deal of the best software you can download is *shareware*; online services are a popular method for distributing this type of software. Shareware is software that you can freely copy and try out, but if you use it for more than a few days, you need to register the software and pay for it. Using shareware has some obvious advantages. You can decide if you like a program before you buy it, and shareware is often less expensive than commercial software.

mirror A duplicate of an FTP site. Mirrors help reduce long-haul Internet traffic by letting people download files from hosts that are closer to them. Usually, mirror sites are updated every night, so that they have the same contents as the main site.

shareware Copyrighted software that you can freely copy and try. If you like and continue to use the software, you must send the author a licensing fee.

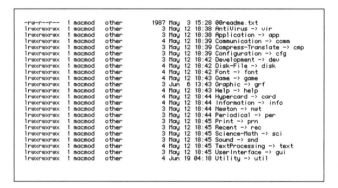

```
-rw-r--r--  1 macmod   other        1987 May  3 15:28 00readme.txt
lrwxrwxrwx  1 macmod   other           3 May 12 18:38 AntiVirus -> vir
lrwxrwxrwx  1 macmod   other           3 May 12 18:38 Application -> app
lrwxrwxrwx  1 macmod   other           4 May 12 18:39 Communication -> comm
lrwxrwxrwx  1 macmod   other           3 May 12 18:39 Compress-Translate -> cmp
lrwxrwxrwx  1 macmod   other           3 May 12 18:39 Configuration -> cfg
lrwxrwxrwx  1 macmod   other           3 May 12 18:42 Development -> dev
lrwxrwxrwx  1 macmod   other           4 May 12 18:42 Disk-File -> disk
lrwxrwxrwx  1 macmod   other           4 May 12 18:42 Font -> font
lrwxrwxrwx  1 macmod   other           4 May 12 18:43 Game -> game
lrwxrwxrwx  1 macmod   other           3 Jun  6 13:43 Graphic -> grf
lrwxrwxrwx  1 macmod   other           4 May 12 18:43 Help -> help
lrwxrwxrwx  1 macmod   other           4 May 12 18:44 Hypercard -> card
lrwxrwxrwx  1 macmod   other           4 May 12 18:44 Information -> info
lrwxrwxrwx  1 macmod   other           3 May 12 18:44 Newton -> nwt
lrwxrwxrwx  1 macmod   other           3 May 12 18:44 Periodical -> per
lrwxrwxrwx  1 macmod   other           3 May 12 18:45 Print -> prn
lrwxrwxrwx  1 macmod   other           3 May 12 18:45 Recent -> rec
lrwxrwxrwx  1 macmod   other           3 May 12 18:45 Science-Math -> sci
lrwxrwxrwx  1 macmod   other           3 May 12 18:45 Sound -> snd
lrwxrwxrwx  1 macmod   other           4 May 12 18:45 TextProcessing -> text
lrwxrwxrwx  1 macmod   other           3 May 12 18:45 UserInterface -> gui
lrwxrwxrwx  1 macmod   other           4 Jun 19 04:18 Utility -> util
```

▶ *Macintosh users have their own archive at Stanford University, called Info-Mac. Even though there are many more PCs than Macintoshes, the Info-Mac archive has almost as many programs as the PC archives. It also has a wealth of informational files, such as instructions for hooking Macintoshes to PC networks.*

```
ftp> cd /pub/etext
250 CWD command successful.
ftp> dir
200 PORT command successful.
150 Opening ASCII mode data connection for /bin/ls.
total 100
-rw-r--r--   1 root     wheel         191 Mar 20  1994 .dir3_0.wmd
-rw-r--r--   1 root     wheel          11 Mar 20  1994 .hidden
-rw-r--r--   1 hart     wheel       27542 Sep 19 09:00 0INDEX.GUT
-rw-r--r--   1 hart     wheel        9189 Jan  1  1994 INDEX100.GUT
-rw-r--r--   1 hart     wheel        5821 Sep  4 07:23 INDEX200.GUT
-rw-r--r--   1 hart     wheel        9214 Jan 15  1990 LIST.COM
-rw-r--r--   1 hart     wheel        4420 Dec  1  1991 NEWUSER.GUT
drwxr-xr-x   3 hart     wheel        1024 Sep  2 19:51 articles
drwxr-xr-x   2 hart     wheel        1024 Dec 10  1993 etext90
drwxr-xr-x   3 hart     wheel        2048 Sep  8 17:03 etext91
drwxr-xr-x   3 hart     wheel        2048 Mar  9  1994 etext92
drwxr-xr-x   2 hart     wheel        4096 Jul 15 16:04 etext93
drwxr-xr-t   4 hart     wheel        4096 Sep 13 10:11 etext94
drwxr-xr-x   2 hart     wheel        1024 Aug  4  1993 freenet
-rw-r--r--   1 hart     wheel       14005 Mar  2  1993 gutmar3.3
drwxr-xr-x   6 hart     wheel        1024 Jan 13  1994 hart
drwxr-xr-x   2 hart     wheel        1024 Nov 30  1993 interpedia
drwxr-xr-x   7 ippe     wheel        1024 Sep 18 10:19 ippe
drwxr-xr-x   2 root     wheel        8192 Mar  1  1994 lost+found
-rw-r--r--   1 hart     wheel         300 Mar 27  1992 note.old
drwxr-xr-x   2 hart     wheel        1024 Oct 25  1991 usonly
226 Transfer complete.
ftp> ▓
```

▶ *Plenty of noncomputer-related files can also be downloaded from the Internet. Project Gutenberg is a collection of literature, mostly classic, that you can get as text files. Hundreds of books are in this collection and more are added every month.*

Business Research

You may think that the best business information is only available in business libraries, but you would be surprised at the wealth of information available on the Internet. Most of it is free, and it is usually available to a wider range of people than standard business data is. The amount of information on the Internet is growing quickly, and the U.S. government is rapidly adding up-to-date business and financial statistics.

Business research usually goes well beyond looking for data, however. For example, you may need to find someone who has expertise in a particular area. Usenet newsgroups are an incredibly valuable resource for contacting experts and locating hard-to-find companies with particular products. If you want to collect information on competing products, you may want to use the World Wide Web, which has an ever-growing selection of catalogs from thousands of vendors and resellers.

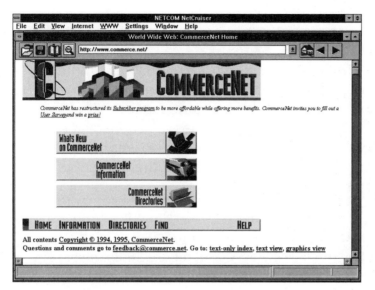

▶ CommerceNet was one of the early leaders in helping companies get established on the World Wide Web. It's working groups are also exploring standards for Internet commerce and researching ways to help businesses find each other.

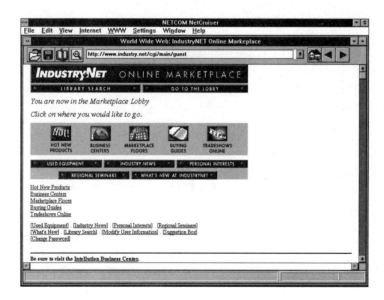

▶ IndustryNET is a free service that is tailored toward the manufacturing industry. It lets companies find suppliers and parts online, as well as giving small companies a way to find suitable partners.

anonymous FTP The use of the FTP program to connect to a host computer on the Internet, access its public directories, and transfer files from the host to your computer. Anonymous FTP is the most common way to search for and download files. Hundreds of host computers on the Internet let anyone use anonymous FTP to look through directories for files they want.

▶ *As you can see, dozens of magazines on different subjects are available from the Internet. This list is from the Gopher server on the WELL, an Internet-based BBS.*

Online Magazines

The Internet is a great medium for publishing magazines. There are no printing costs, very few real costs, and distribution is quite easy. If your magazine is popular, tens of thousands of people read each issue. For all of these reasons, dozens of small magazines have appeared on the Internet in the past few years.

Many online magazines are about computers, but many are not. Some aren't magazines as much as they are newsletters about a particular subject. The more effort and time the editor of the magazine puts into it, and the more contributions that come in from readers, the better the magazine.

There are many places to get magazines on the Internet. Many are distributed by anonymous FTP, particularly the ones about computers. Others are distributed through mailing lists and appear in mailboxes periodically. Some magazines are distributed only through the World Wide Web. Because of the large number of magazines and the many ways in which they are distributed, many lists of online magazines are available.

Don't assume that just because a magazine is online that the information isn't as good or as newsy as in printed magazines. Some of the best investigative journalism today is found in online magazines. Because it is inexpensive to start an online magazine, a single good writer can create a great publication without worrying about the overhead of printing, subscriptions, and so on. Also, online magazines often get much better response from their readers than printed magazines do, so the letters sections in online magazines are often more interesting.

FAQs

Many Usenet newsgroups cover how-to topics, which is great, but many first-time Usenet users ask the same basic questions. For people who read the newsgroup every day for years, such questions become tiresome and just waste space. Many years ago, busy newsgroups began creating lists of FAQs, or frequently asked questions and, of course, their answers.

FAQ files can be some of the most useful documents you will ever read. They are usually either written by one person who knows a lot or compiled by someone with the help of many other people. FAQs are often reposted to the newsgroup every two weeks in order to help newcomers find the information they need without having to ask the same question that may have been recently answered.

One of the best features of FAQs is that they are often updated. This is useful for computer-related topics that change all the time, as well as for newsgroups that cover television shows, sports, and other entertainment. When you first read a Usenet newsgroup, you should see if there is an FAQ file list and if it has been posted recently.

FAQs are not only useful for when you read Usenet newsgroups. For example, you might be interested in getting rid of your pet's

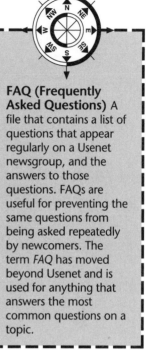

FAQ (Frequently Asked Questions) A file that contains a list of questions that appear regularly on a Usenet newsgroup, and the answers to those questions. FAQs are useful for preventing the same questions from being asked repeatedly by newcomers. The term *FAQ* has moved beyond Usenet and is used for anything that answers the most common questions on a topic.

Usenet A widely used Internet service that organizes people's comments by topic. These topics, called newsgroups, have their own structure, with people commenting on previous comments and starting new discussions. Usenet is the second most popular Internet feature, after mail.

fleas, but not really interested in reading the pet-related Usenet newsgroups. You can, and should, still pick up the pet-related FAQ and use the information in it. If you find something in the FAQ that is not correct or you can add to, consider reading the newsgroup regularly and contributing to the FAQ. Incidentally, a few mailing lists also have FAQ files, although they are often more difficult to find.

Sample FAQs

Many of the best FAQs have nothing to do with computers. Here are some pearls of wisdom from a few of the hundreds of Usenet FAQ files.

From the Disneyland FAQ

Crossing a parade route is possible, but time-consuming. Certain areas are marked for crossing and guests are allowed to cross during gaps in the parade. Plan which side of the park you want to be on during the parade and get there early. If you must cross, consider using the Disneyland RR or the Skyway. Parade crossing zones north of the Matterhorn are usually less congested than the one at the Hub. Main Street is tough (though not impossible) to negotiate during popular parades.

From the fleas and ticks FAQ

A good preventive method is to put down towels everywhere your pet normally lies and then wash those towels once a week. Deposited flea eggs are therefore cleaned out regularly. Regular vacuuming and emptying of the vacuum bag also helps, independently of any method or methods you choose to use because that eliminates or reduces food sources for the larvae.

From the disc (as in Frisbee) FAQ

So, what does this all mean? In terms of flight dynamics, the small displacement given to the disc by the thumb at the last second causes the leading edge to rise. This, in combination with the large, instantaneous, simultaneous forward force of the throw (called the impulse) creates a high angle of attack flight regime, with the possibility of an increase in altitude, depending on the actual angle of release from the hand.

From the tattoo FAQ

What sorts of things to look for in a tattoo shop

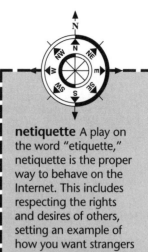

netiquette A play on the word "etiquette," netiquette is the proper way to behave on the Internet. This includes respecting the rights and desires of others, setting an example of how you want strangers to treat you, and acknowledging that the Internet is very different from face-to-face communication.

▶ Looking critically at the shop is as important as choosing your artist. Make sure the place is very clean, make sure the artist uses an autoclave or uses disposable needles (or both). Don't be afraid to ask, either.

▶ What does the shop look like? What is its ambiance? Does it look like a barber shop, a hair salon, a dental office, or an art gallery? If you are a nonsmoker, will cigarette smoke bother you? Look for used ashtrays as signs. Do the work areas offer you any privacy? Do they use shower curtains, private booths, or shoulder-high room dividers?

Games, Sports, and Hobbies

One of the great features of the World Wide Web is all the people who create centralized locations for finding information about particular topics. Leisure is a popular discussion topic on the Internet, almost as popular as discussions about computers. Hundreds of Usenet newsgroups cover different types of activities that

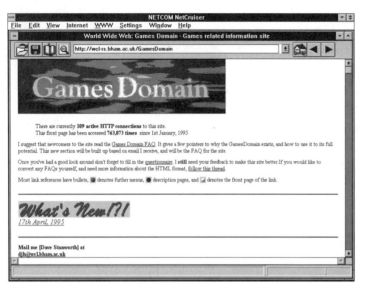

▶ *This is the Games Domain, a Web site in England, where you can find lists of Usenet newsgroups and FAQ files that relate to game playing.*

people do when they're not working or talking politics. Many World Wide Web sites also relate to hobbies and sports as well.

It seems people like to talk about playing games as much as they like to play them. Most of the Usenet newsgroups about games are under the *rec* hierarchy, but many also appear in *alt* and *comp*. For example, some of the news groups with games include

▶ **rec.gambling** is a general discussion of gambling, gaming for money, places for gambling, and so on.

▶ **rec.games.backgammon** covers backgammon and **rec.games.board** covers all types of board games, including some old classics.

▶ **rec.games.bridge** and **rec.games.chess** cover some other classics.

▶ **rec.games.design** is a very active discussion of how to design new games, both electronic and standard.

▶ **rec.games.frp** is a hierarchy of topics about fantasy and role-playing games.

▶ **rec.games.miniatures** is for people who like to create and paint miniature models for their game playing.

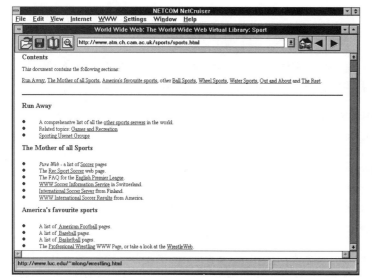

▶ Another British Web page is the Sports index for the World Wide Web Virtual Library. Note how non-U.S. sports get top billing on the page. Many people forget that the Internet is international. When it comes to sports, what is called soccer in the U.S. is by far more popular in Great Britain than football or baseball.

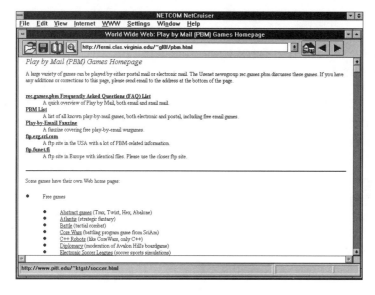

▶ Some people even like playing games through the mail. "Play By Mail" games have been around for decades using postal mail, but the advent of Internet mail has made them easier and faster to play. These games usually give each player lots of time to think about his or her next move and therefore aren't as frenetic as other popular games.

▶ **rec.games.pinball** proves that those machines will never die.

▶ **rec.games.programmer** is another lively discussion, specifically for people programming new games.

▶ **rec.games.video** all types of video games, such as Nintendo, Sega, Atari, and arcade games.

If you start reading some of the Usenet newsgroups relating to games, sports, and hobbies, you may become intimidated by the expertise of some of the other people posting messages. Try to remember three important things:

▶ Everyone who posts on the newsgroup started out as a beginner. They may sound quite professional now, but they weren't always.

▶ For every person who posts, at least ten only read. Many of the people who don't say anything are novices who are just trying to get tips and ideas.

▶ It's your interest in the hobby or sport that matters. Feel free to be as much of a beginner as you want. You're here to enjoy yourself.

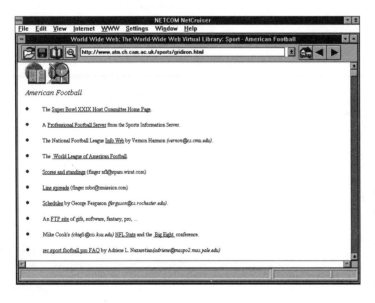

▶ As you would expect, the Internet is the place to get statistics about most professional sports. Given the large university community on the Internet, there are lots of college sports statistics as well.

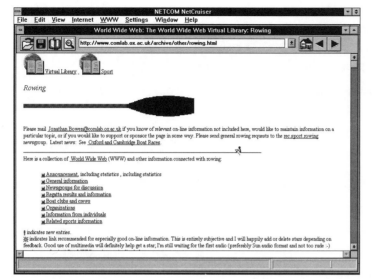

▶ *The Internet also covers many less popular sports, such as rowing. In fact, the Usenet newsgroups for less popular sports are often more interesting than the ones for the most popular sports because people in the discussions are often actively involved with the sport.*

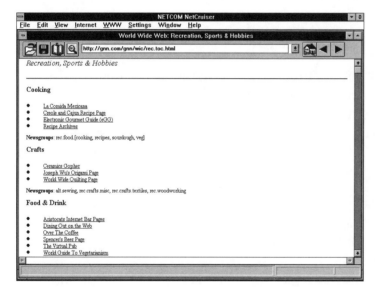

▶ *There are Usenet news groups for almost every hobby, and there are some non-Usenet resources as well. Here are some of the hobby-related topics, as described in the Global Network Navigator.*

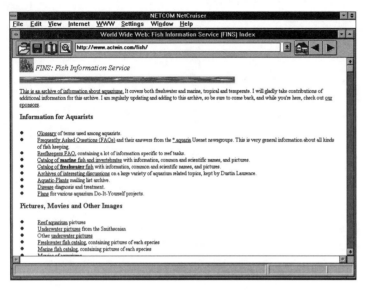

▶ *If you keep fish, there is extensive information on aquaria, types of fish, foods, and so on. The previous experience of other people with the same interests is often the most useful information you can have about your hobby.*

News and Views

The Internet is more than just an information center: it is also a great place to meet and chat with people. Mind you, "meet" in this case usually means getting together only on the Internet because most of the time, people who converse on the Internet never meet face to face (or *F2F* as it is sometimes called). But the meetings seem just as real.

You can chat in many different ways. There are the IRC areas, where the chatting is in real time and often hard to follow. Dozens of Usenet newsgroups, mostly in the *soc.* and *talk.* hierarchies, have discussions about everything from politics to recipes. And many mailing lists are also good places to find people with similar interests.

The goal of talking is not just to convince other people that you are right. It is also a good way to hear the views of others, and to find people who interest you in order to talk about other things. Many friendships have been made by people starting discussions in the *talk.* newsgroups. The current *talk.* groups include the following:

- talk.abortion
- talk.answers
- talk.bizarre
- talk.bizarre.nice
- talk.environment
- talk.origins
- talk.philosophy.misc
- talk.politics.animals
- talk.politics.china
- talk.politics.cis
- talk.politics.crypto
- talk.politics.drugs
- talk.politics.guns
- talk.politics.medicine
- talk.politics.mideast
- talk.politics.misc
- talk.politics.soviet
- talk.politics.theory
- talk.politics.tibet
- talk.rape
- talk.religion.misc
- talk.religion.newage
- talk.rumors

The newsgroups in the *soc.* hierarchy are usually more cultural than those in *talk*. Also, the discussions here often are more first-person, because thousands of people on the Internet come from the backgrounds discussed in the groups. Some of the *soc.* groups include

- **soc.answers** collects all the FAQ files for all the *soc.* groups.
- **soc.bi** discusses bisexuality.
- **soc.college** is a general discussion of university life.
- **soc.couples** covers issues that come up for couples, such as marriage, divorce, families, and so on.
- **soc.culture** is a hierarchy with dozens of specific cultures represented. The discussions here include art, music, travel, and so on for people all over the world.

▶ **soc.feminism**

▶ **soc.men**

▶ **soc.motss** is a discussion of lesbian and gay issues. (motss is an acronym for "members of the same sex.")

▶ **soc.org.nonprofit**

▶ **soc.penpals**

▶ **soc.politics** is a wide-ranging group discussion about a lot, and not much, at the same time.

▶ **soc.religion** is another large hierarchy that covers many major world religions.

▷	3	David Caswell	Re: man and women
▷	12	Sandworm1	Re: NLP is like Lifespring, EST, the Forum....
▷	21	Mark J. Baker	Smoking? Turn-off?
▷	3	Kenneth Roy S...	Re: Great sex or great food? (Was: Like water for chocolate)
▷	6	Lauren Holmes	Eduardo's own subject line (Was Re: Lewis De Payne.)
-		Phillip J. Birmi...	Eduardo's own chatter-guitar theme music.
▷	2	Brandon Sonde...	Hey, I wanted to post something cool, but my roomate gave me a hack.
▷	3	Wicked	Re: Debbie does FAKITA
-		Michael Sulliv...	semi-moderation? (was Re: Lewis De Payne.)
-		Eduardo Cordei...	Phillip is getting there (was Re: Referring to women as "ladies")
-		Eduardo Cordei...	You guys want "slobbering"? (was Re: Late night phone calls
-		Seth Breidbart	Re: Gifted programs (was re boredom)
▷	4	betty boop	Social Subjects Wanted for Baudy Book
▷	2	Stef Jones	Psycho babble (Was: Late night phone calls)
-		Michael Sulliv...	semi-moderation cabal (was Re: Lewis De Payne.)
▷	9	Darrin Rodrigu...	First thing women Look for?
▷	6	Sandworm1	The ethics of covert seduction....
▷	10	Lewis De Payne	Old Time Net Seduction
▷	6	Chris Bradley	I don't get it...
-		piranha	Re: Happened today
-		5419@delphi.co...	Singles in Phoenix/Scottsdale area?
▷	3	Chris Neil Hur...	What is your source of amusement?
-		data@gsp.com	< ARE YOU LOOKING FOR THE RIGHT PERSON TO CONVERSE WITH? >
-		mike jourard	Dating & Coffee
-		Michael Sulliv...	Boycott lewis. don't follow-up (wasRe: PROPOSAL: MODERATION-BOT)
-		Michael Sulliv...	Boycott lewis. don't follow-up (was Re: Master of Triplicate Forms to the FBI!)
▷	6	Po-Han Lin	Hunter, Gatherer
-		Michael Sulliv...	Please Ignore Lewis (was Re: Old Time Net Seduction)
-		Stef Jones	Possession! (Was: You guys want "slobbering"?)

▶ *As you can see, the topics on the "soc.singles" Usenet newsgroup is about almost anything, not just being single. However, there is certainly lots of singles-specific talk as well, not unlike any large singles meeting.*

- soc.singles
- soc.veterans
- soc.women

Many stories of people meeting friends and even spouses on the Internet abound. To people who don't use the Internet, this may seem really strange, because you don't get to see the other person or even hear what they sound like. On the other hand, if you think about how you have met some of your other friends over your lifetime, the idea of meeting people online doesn't sound so weird. Many Internet users find that they get to know the most important parts of a person best — and first — on the Internet, and things such as looks and accents don't get in the way there.

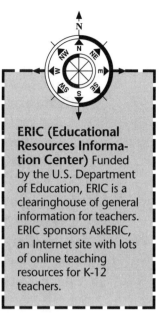

ERIC (Educational Resources Information Center) Funded by the U.S. Department of Education, ERIC is a clearinghouse of general information for teachers. ERIC sponsors AskERIC, an Internet site with lots of online teaching resources for K-12 teachers.

K-12 Resources

The Internet has been well received by the education community for many years. The main educational uses of the Internet so far include

- Helping teachers exchange information and lesson plans
- Letting children interact with other kids outside of their school
- Allowing students new ways to do research papers and reports

As more and more schools begin using the Internet, the number and kinds of applications will expand greatly. Fortunately, there are central places that collect information for teachers and parents about Internet resources for education. One of the best known starting places is AskERIC, which is part of ERIC, the Educational Resources Information Center of the U.S. Department of Education.

Many of the K-12 resources aren't just for schools. Instead, they come from local community groups who help kids in all areas of their lives, including staying in school.

▶ *AskERIC is a great resource for teachers and parents.*

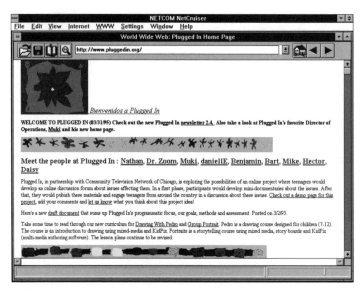

▶ *Plugged In is a community group that teaches low-income children about using computers.*

College Libraries

Over the past two decades, tens of millions of dollars have been spent automating the card catalogs of university libraries throughout the United States. Given the size of the collections in many of these libraries, computerizing them made great sense. One of the biggest benefits of computerizing these card catalogs is that many libraries realized they could let outsiders use their libraries without draining their computers' resources.

Being able to search a college library's catalog is a very useful research tool. Even if you never set foot in the library, you can learn a great deal from the catalog. For example, you can find out if a book about a particular topic exists and get the relevant information on the book. Or, you can start a research project on a particular subject and have a good idea of what kind of material is available on the topic.

Most libraries that let outside users peruse their catalogs do so through the telnet program. This means that the program you use to look for books is character based. The programs are also usually quite old; some of them were written in the late 1970s and have never really been updated since then. There is no *single* interface to the catalogs; in fact, there are dozens.

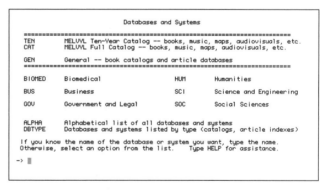

▶ *This is a typical screen from a college library catalog. Note that the interface is almost always character based because the libraries use the telnet program — which is character based — to grant access to users.*

Hytelnet A program that works with telnet to let you easily browse through library catalogs. Hytelnet has a database of all known public library catalogs and information about how to operate them when you are connected to them.

Hundreds of libraries make their catalogs available on the Internet. The best way to find out which libraries have such access is through a program called *Hytelnet*, which acts as a front end to telnet. Hytelnet lists all known catalogs. A few libraries have converted their interfaces to Gopher and the World Wide Web, but they are in the minority, leaving users with having to learn a new program for each different catalog they use.

Government Information

An area of the Internet that has had a great deal of activity recently is public access to government information. Interest is particularly strong in the United States, but Internet users in other countries have been affected as well. Because most governments already have a great deal of public information in databases, many people feel that they should make it freely available to anyone who can access the Internet.

In the United States, the government is split into three branches: executive, legislative, and judicial. The exectutive branch usually consists of elected administrators (such as "president@whitehouse.gov," governors, and mayors), as well as the various police forces; the legislative branch includes elected representatives; and the judicial branch covers the courts. As you may imagine, all three branches usually have a wealth of records and documents that significantly impacts everyone's daily lives, and most of that information was collected using public funds.

Thus, thousands of people want to make government information more easily accessed by all citizens, not just lawyers and other people with legal training. For example, imagine if you could read the text of an upcoming bill instead of just reading some politician's quotes about the bill in the newspaper. Further, imagine if you could easily determine whether an incumbent governor had vetoed or supported various bills that concern you in the last year. Easy access to these records over the Internet could revolutionize the way we interact with our government.

Many states have started to put some of their laws, administrative decisions, and judicial decisions online. California is at the forefront, due in no small part to Internet activists who are also part of the computer industry.

CALIFORNIA RESOURCES

- California Gophers
- California Libraries
- Virtual Tourist - California
  - Fantastic list of all California businesses, events, tourist attractions!
- Association of Bay Area Governments
- California Codes
- California Elections Results, June 7, 1994
- California Government Sources of Electronic Information (Mays)
- California Legislature via Gopher, World Wide Web, or UC Santa Cruz
  - Search by bill number or topic
- California Secretary of State
- California State Government Network
- Geographical Server
- Governor's Office of Emergency Services
  - Weather and road reports for California
- Los Angeles Free Net
- Newspapers - California
- Silicon Valley Public Access Link
- Southern California Online User's Group (SCOUG)

Return to Buddies Menu

▶ *California is at the forefront of the move to make government information available online.*

Vehicle Code

GENERAL PROVISIONS 1-32

DIVISION 1. WORDS AND PHRASES DEFINED 100-680

DIVISION 2. ADMINISTRATION

▶ *This is the table of contents for the California Vehicle Code. You might use this if you get a traffic ticket and want to look up the full wording of the law you are accused of breaking.*

For example, all of California's state laws are available through the World Wide Web.

The U.S. federal government is also moving toward open access of some federal records, and many administrative branches of the federal government are making client information available over the Internet. For example, agencies such as the Social Security Administration, which has tens of millions of regular clients, have already put a great deal of information on the Internet.

Of course, many government officials are not particularly happy about this trend in making government information more accessible. The trend is certainly here, however, and the first steps to making this kind of information easily available to everyone are being taken on federal, state, and local levels throughout the United States. In the next few years, the number of sites for all levels of government will probably increase greatly.

United States Government Servers

There are several sites maintaining lists of U.S. Government Servers and Information. See U.S. Government Resources for a fairly complete list. Also check GNN's Govt. & Politics page.

> State Government Information
> U.S. Government Hypertexts
>> From Sunsite at UNC
> List of U.S. Govt. Online Service Providers
>> Also see U.S. Government Laboratories
> United States Census Bureau
> U.S. Code of Federal Regulations (gopher)
> U.S. Department of Commerce
> U.S. Declaration of Independence
> U.S. Department of Education (ED)
> U.S. Department of Energy's Office of Environment, Safety and Health (EH)
> Federal Communications Commission (gopher)
> U.S. Federal Register
> U.S. Geological Survey
> U.S. Senate Gopher
> U.S. Congressional Legislation (telnet)
>> Updated Daily A WAIS index of the text of all bills in the 103rd Congress is now available.
> Congressional Research Service
>> Login as "guest" with password "visitor"

▶ *This is a partial list of the kinds of U.S. government information you can find on the Internet, for free, today. Note that many other records are available for a fee (which is often high), and many of those records are being converted to free access.*

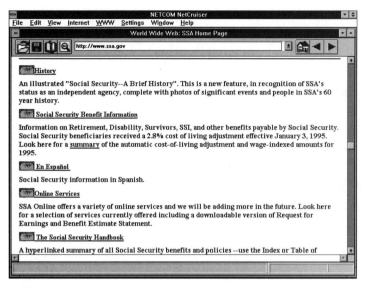

▶ *This is the Social Security Administration's home page.*

▶ *The United States is not alone in putting governmental information on the Internet. This is part of a Web site at the University of Salzburg in Austria that covers Austrian law and politics.*

Gopher A menu-based service that lets you easily find information on the Internet. Gopher presents all information as either a directory or a file, and most Gopher servers let you search for information as well. More than 1,000 Gopher servers are available on the Internet, and Gopher client programs exist for almost every computer.

World Wide Web (WWW) An Internet service that lets users retrieve hypertext and graphics from various sites. Often called just "the Web," the World Wide Web has become one of the most popular Internet services in the past two years. In fact, many Internet information providers publish using only the Web.

[Topics Index] . [Linkages Home]

The United Nations Commission on Sustainable Development (CSD)

Online Resources

The United Nations Commission on Sustainable Development was created by the UN General Assembly through resolution A/47/191 "Institutional arrangements to follow up the United Nations Conference on Environment and Development" in December 1992. The CSD was established to develop mechanisms for effective review and monitoring of the implementation of Agenda 21 and the other Rio agreements, to enhance international cooperation and the rationalize the intergovernmental decision-making capacity for the integration of environment and development issues.

The CSD has had two sessions: from 14-25 June 1993; and 16-27 May 1994. Information on the CSD can be found in Volume Five of the Earth Negotiations Bulletin.

The CSD has had two sessions: from 14-25 June 1993; and 16-27 May 1994. Also, the CSD held two *ad hoc* open-ended working groups on financial flows and mechanism and technology transfer and cooperation, which met from 22 February to 2 March 1994.

The UNDP gopher has some information from the Second Substantive Session including the official UN documentation, the government statements, the statements by representatives of UN agencies, statements by representatives of some NGOs and copies of ECO published at this session of the CSD. Of the more notable speeches are: Under-Secretary-General Nitin Desai's opening speech; the new Chair of the CSD Klaus Topfer's opening speech; and the speech presented by the outgoing Chair, Ismail Razali.

▶ *Thousands of nongovernmental organizations have a say in day-to-day politics around the world, and many of them also have information servers on the Internet. In addition, many branches of the United Nations are starting Gopher and Web sites.*

Travel

You can use the Internet in many ways to help you plan vacation or business travel. You can find a wealth of information about various destinations in many different parts of the Internet. For example, many Gopher sites at universities also have local information.

Many travel-related Usenet newsgroups are in the "rec.travel" hierarchy. You can often also get good information from some of the local hierarchies of the locations you will be traveling to. The current topics include

▶ **rec.travel**

▶ **rec.travel.air**

▶ **rec.travel.asia**

- rec.travel.cruises
- rec.travel.europe
- rec.travel.marketplace
- rec.travel.misc
- rec.travel.usa-canada
- alt.travel.road-trip

Some people use the Usenet newsgroups to get a feeling for a country or city before they travel there, while others use them to find suggestions for restaurants and hotels

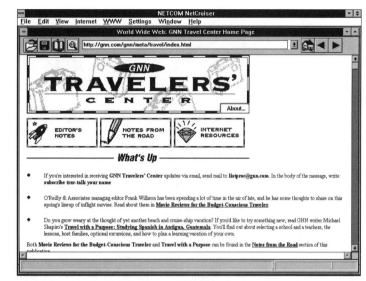

▶ The Travelers' Center on the Global Network Navigator is a great starting place for travel-related searching. You can find articles on specific locations, maps, weather reports, and so on.

that aren't listed in the travel books. This is particularly useful if you like to eat in or stay at smaller or less well-known places. For example, if you really like Chinese food, low-cost Chinese restaurants are rarely listed in travel books; posting a message on the Usenet newsgroup for information about your travel destination often yields the name of the best low-cost restaurant in town.

You can occasionally find similar information on Gopher and World Wide Web servers that are located where you are going. Some universities, and a few cities, have begun setting up servers to encourage tourism or just because it is fun. These servers often do not list as much information as a good guide book, but they are usually more current and might include a list of upcoming events such as festivals, concerts, and so on. If nothing else, the Gopher or Web server will probably give you the address of the tourist information bureau for you to visit when you first arrive at your destination.

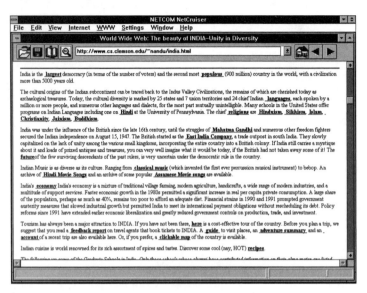

▶ *Another great feature of the Travelers' Center is the long descriptions of individual destinations by individuals who have visited those destinations. For example, this description of India gives great advice that you would not normally find in the traditional travel book.*

Jobs and Careers

Searching for employment is never easy, but the Internet can come to your aid and certainly make it easier. Many servers on the Internet have current job listings, and you can often use Internet mail to communicate directly with companies that are offering jobs.

The Online Career Center is just one of the many Gopher and Web servers that you can browse for job listings. Some of these servers are run by newspapers, others by private companies. Of course, there is no single, central place to look for a job, but with a few hours of poking around, you can probably find many interesting listings.

The place many people look first for new job listings is the Usenet "misc.jobs.offered" newsgroup. Although the job you want may not be listed there, you might find which companies in your area have many jobs available and follow up with them about the one you want.

The *Chronicle of Higher Education* is probably the most central place to look for jobs at colleges and universities. Its Gopher server has a searchable list of the job listings in a recent issue of the weekly, as well as the online version of many of the articles from that issue as well.

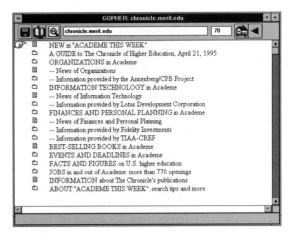

▶ *The* Chronicle of Higher Education *Gopher server is another useful resource for job seekers.*

-	N. Riccione	C++, Unix, Motif, Telecom, Dallas, TX
-	hac@epx.cis.u...	ECAD/CAE Software Development Eng., Supercomputers (Chippewa Falls, ...
-	hac@epx.cis.u...	IC Design Eng., Full Custom CMOS Supercomputers (Cray in Chippewa Falls...
-	hac@epx.cis.u...	Processor Architecture and Design Eng., Full Custom CMOS (Chippewa Falls,...
-	hac@epx.cis.u...	Sr. IC Design Engineer, Full Custom CMOS Supercomputers (Chippewa Falls...
-	hac@epx.cis.u...	Supercomputer Presales Systems Engineer (Detroit area)
-	hac@epx.cis.u...	MESH GENERATION Specialist, Mechanical CAD/CAE (Michigan)
-	hac@epx.cis.u...	Crash Analysis Analyst/Programmer - (Ann Arbor, MI)
-	hac@epx.cis.u...	IBM Large Systems Software Developer (Minneapolis)
-	Ian O'Keefe	OK#35:Designer:TX:UNIX:RPC:DME:Client Server
-	Ian O'Keefe	#OK7:P/A:TX:Data Analysis:Data Modeling:ERDs:DB2:Pacbase
-	Ian O'Keefe	#OK6:PA position:TX:Assembly:ALC:Lifecom:Life70:Vantage
-	Ian O'Keefe	#OK17:Project Mgr:TX:OS/2:Workplace Shell:C++:OOP
-	Ian O'Keefe	#OK3:C++:Unix:Algorithm:Math:Tx
-	Al Will	Dallas: Senior Smalltalk Programmer
-	Dave Whipple	TELECOMMUNICATIONS ENGINEERS/MCI/Cary, NC
-	Karen Stinnett	Networking SW Development Engineer, Convex Computer Corp., Richards...
-	Perii Systems	Pro/Engineer Cad System
-	Perii Systems	Software Developer
-	Perii Systems	Programmer Analyst
-	Karen Stinnett	Operating Systems Development Engineer, Convex Computer Corp., Richar...
-	J. Becker @ OCTS	Telecommunications Manager
-	Larry Cohen	Sybase DBA, NYC Financial
-	Larry Cohen	Systems Administration, NYC Financial
-	Jobs offered	Jr. Programmer (Macintosh) @ U. Chicago, Chicago, Illinois USA
-	Larry Cohen	C++ Applications, NYC Financial
-	Joe Montgomery	System Admin (Unix/Netware)
-	Mark Grand	Looking for the World Best Fish (Buyer) - Atlanta, GA
-	Robert M Kofoed	REAL-TIME 68000 DEVELOPERS NJ

▶ *The Usenet "misc.jobs.offered" newsgroup is a good place to check for job listings.*

▶ *Online Career Center main menu*

Commercial Internet Sites

Despite myths to the contrary, the Internet has been used for commercial purposes for almost as long as it has existed. UNIX hardware and software companies have had advertising and customer support on the Internet for more than a decade, and in the past five years, many companies have used the Usenet news groups to announce new products.

Today, the Internet is growing rapidly based on users' expectations of finding great information quickly. Some of that information is inherently commercial. For example, if you want to know what brand of drawing software performs a specific kind of task, getting the answer to that query is a commercial use of the Internet.

```
Q

363. Quadralay Corporation, software development tools
     •  Quadralay MarketPlace
     •  Austin, TX information
364. Qualitative Solutions & Research Pty/Ltd (6/6/94)
365. Quality Micro Systems Inc. (QMS) manufacturer of print systems
366. Quarderdeck Office Systems (5/16/94)
367. QuoteCom, stock quotes (6/6/94, also 7/20/94)

R

368. The Racquet Workshop, specialty tennis shoppe (7/30/94)
369. Racal-Datacom Corporate Headquarters Home Page (8/5/94)
370. Raven Systems Ltd., custom software solutions for everyday problems (6/13/94)
371. The Real Estate Network (9/4/94)
372. RealTech Systems Corporation (9/4/94)
373. Real/Time Communications, Internet access provider, Austin, Texas (5/11/94)
374. Reasoning Systems, code analysis and transformation tools for evaluating, maintaining and reengineering Ada, C,
     COBOL and FORTRAN.
375. The Reference Press Business Handbooks (5/11/94)
376. Research Access Incorporated (8/28/94)
377. Resolution Buisness Press, Inc. (8/28/94)
378. Rhonda Francis Communications (9/15/94)
```

▶ *Literally thousands of companies have a presence on the Internet. You can use lists of commercial sites, such as this one maintained at MIT, to keep up on the latest company information.*

This is true regardless of whether the answer comes from a satisfied customer or from the company that makes the software.

Companies have been experimenting with commercial use of the Internet in many different ways. The most direct method is for a company to have a Web or Gopher server that contains advertising for its products. Another common method is for a company to create a file response system or a mailing list to mail product information. Some companies also provide interesting free information that is not directly related to their products and then hope to make a good impression by sponsoring that information.

Ordering online is becoming more popular. For example, one of the first noncomputer-related commercial vendors on the Web was Grant's Florist and Greenhouse, which called its service the Internet Flower Shop.

If you think about it, the process is not much different than looking in a print catalog and ordering over the phone. However, if you don't have the catalog handy, or if the dealer changes the arrangement in the print catalog, you aren't really sure what you've ordered. With an online catalog, you can be sure you are getting the latest version.

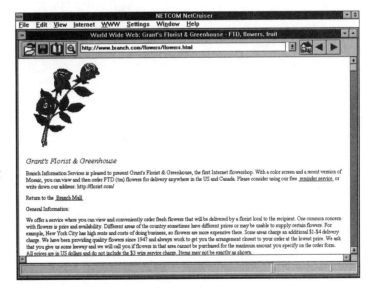

▶ *The Internet Flower Shop.*

CIX (Commercial Internet Exchange) The first major industry group for companies that provide Internet access. Because CIX consists of competitors in a constantly changing market, it is a somewhat volatile group. CIX also lobbies the U.S. government on Internet-related issues.

host On the Internet, and other networks, a host is the computer that performs centralized functions. For example, a host makes program or data files available to computers on the Internet.

server In client/server network architecture, a single, high-powered machine with a huge hard disk set aside to function as a file server for all the client machines in the network.

There is much more to the commercial Internet than just ordering merchandise, however. A radio station, for example, may use its Web server as a way to let listeners find more information about the music the station plays, to talk about its DJs, and so on.

Another type of service company beginning to advertise on the Internet is law firms. Using a Gopher or Web server, these firms can list the specialties of their clients, talk about well-known clients, and so on.

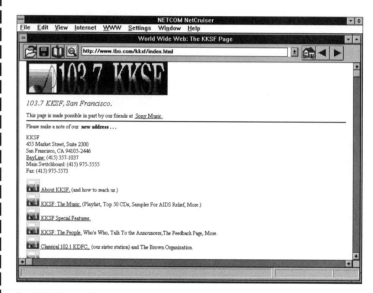

▶ *KKSF's Web page.*

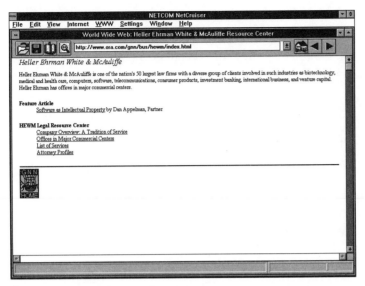

▶ *A typical law firm Web page.*

Humor

Humor certainly depends on individual tastes, but almost anyone can find lots to laugh about on the Internet. Many people have set up centers of jokes and other funny bits that can lighten up your day when you need a bit of a chuckle.

If you're in the mood for a few jokes, you might want to take a look at the "rec.humor" and "rec.humor.funny" Usenet news groups. "rec.humor" is a free-for-all, while "rec.humor.funny" is moderated and gets only a few jokes a week.

A few examples from Usenet:

▶ Q: What's the definition of an election?

A: An advance auction of stolen goods.

▶ Two friends of mine were traveling between San Diego and Utah on obscure roads rather than the normal I-15 route when they came across a hand-painted sign at the side of the road that said:

No Cops — Floor It

About the time the speedometer hit 120 mph, they saw another sign that wasn't hand painted. Much to their dismay, it said:

Pavement Ends 500 feet.

▶ Seen on a license plate frame: "Horn broken, watch for finger."

▶ A true story of dumb things you can say:

Last year, I attended a lecture by Stephen Hawking at which he talked about computers and their potential for artificial intelligence. He had a definition of "life" that included computer viruses, and this definition stuck in my mind. A few days later, as I was describing the lecture to my parents and aunt and uncle, I came to the part about computer viruses. I keep my computer in my bedroom, and I suppose many other people do, too, so it was in complete innocence that I proclaimed:

"Imagine! You can now create life in your own bedroom!"

Everyone stared at me when I said that, and the full meaning of what I had just said was just starting to sink in when my mom confided, "That's usually the way it works."

The Internet is the home of an interesting experiment in interactive humor. The Usenet Oracle is a place for people to ask questions (sometimes serious, sometimes not) and get answers (always humorous). Anyone can ask or answer a question, although the answers have a particular style that has evolved over time.

The newsgroup where the answers are posted, "rec.humor.oracle" is moderated, so only the best question-and-answer pairs are posted. Because anyone can be the Oracle for the moment when answering questions, the type of humor you see is wide ranging.

```
The Usenet Oracle has pondered your question deeply.
Your question was:

> Oh racle
> how do you prove the Final-value Theorem,
>
> i.e.    lim    f(t)  =  lim   sF(s)
>              t->inf            s->0

And in response, thus spake the Oracle:

}         The Final-value theorem has caused much consternation among
} students throughout the ages, because most calculus professors refuse
} to discuss the actual origin of the Theorem. You will notice that we
} are calculating limits, more specifically, Visa credit card limits.

}         lim f(t) = lim sF(s)
}              t->inf      s->0
}
}         This equation calculates how much you pay each month as your
} credit line (t) approaches infinity, and your minimum payment (s)
} approaches nothing. This is the equation that allows the bank to
} generate vast sums by allowing you to overstretch your income, charging
} really cool stuff, and paying over time.
}         Escape while you can! Pay cash!!
}
} You owe the Oracle $488 to cover his AmEx bill.

--------------------------------

The Usenet Oracle has pondered your question deeply.
Your question was:

> If moths are attracted to light, why do they not fly towards the sun?

And in response, thus spake the Oracle:

} Where do you think moths go during the day?
```

▶ *An example of the questions and answers you might see in "rec.humor.oracle."*

PART 5

Searching for Information on the Internet

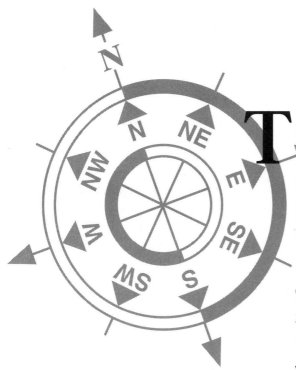

The Internet is already vast and is growing every day. Finding information or people on the Internet is often pretty difficult because of the sheer size of the Internet. Fortunately, many good tools are available for searching different parts of the Internet to find the information you want.

Veronica

When you want to find a particular subject on a Gopher server, Veronica is the place to go. The *Veronica* database has the names of almost all of the directories and files on every public Gopher server in the world. Of course, you reach Veronica through Gopher.

After you connect to one of the many Veronica servers throughout the world, you enter a word or phrase for your search. Veronica searches the database and gives you a list of all the entries that match your search. Using special keywords, you can limit your search to particular kinds of files, or just look for directory names with the text you want. This is useful if you are looking for particular kinds of information, such as collections of class notes.

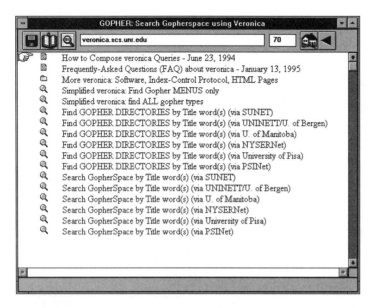

▶ You can connect to many different Veronica servers. They often have the same database, but not always. Also, some have added different options for the kinds of information you get back. Generally, you should choose the Veronica server closest to you.

▶ Searching Veronica for a single word often yields dozens or hundreds of matching items. Here, the name "Nixon" was used to get quite a long list of items. You could narrow the search by looking for "Nixon" and "Watergate" in the same entry.

You may wonder how Veronica got its name. First there was Archie, the database that tells you the contents of many of the FTP archives around the world. Although Archie was named as an abbreviation for the word *archive*, when the developers of Veronica had to choose a name, they thought of the popular comic books. Supposedly, Veronica stands for Very Easy Rodent-Oriented Netwide Index to Computerized Archives, but that is really stretching the idea just a bit far.

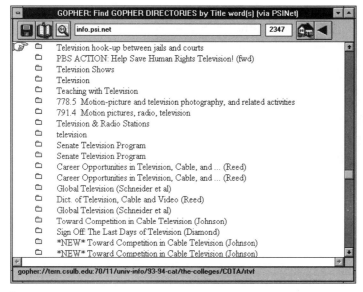

gopher://tern.csulb.edu:70/11/univ-info/93-94-cat/the-colleges/COTA/rtvf

▶ *You can specify that you just want to see Gopher directories, not files, with the particular word. In this case, Veronica searched for all directories with the word "television."*

Gopher A menu-based service that lets you easily find information on all kinds of subjects. Gopher presents all information as either a directory or a file, and most Gopher servers let you search for information as well. More than 1,000 Gopher servers are available on the Internet, and Gopher client programs exist for almost every computer.

Veronica A service that searches for files on Gopher servers. You use a Gopher client to access a Veronica server, and then send Veronica a search request. Veronica servers can give you answers in a variety of ways, such as by listing only directories that match your request.

Archie

Archie (from archive) is to FTP what Veronica is to Gopher. Archie is a database of hundreds of thousands of files that you can download through anonymous FTP. You access the Archie database from one of the Archie servers on the Internet by using either character-based telnet or a special Archie client.

One of the most difficult problems with using Archie is finding an Archie server that responds to your requests. There are over a dozen such servers, but sending Archie requests to them often yields no results. This is partially due to the number of people sending Archie requests, and partially due to restrictions that the administrators at the servers have made regarding how much of the host Archie can take.

Unfortunately, Archie has the same limitations that anonymous FTP does. Because the filenames on the Internet are not usually very descriptive, searching for something when you don't know its name is hit and miss. You can make many guesses, but FTP files aren't as well named as Gopher entries, so you can't be sure that you can find what you want.

Name	Size	Date	Zone	Host
47.10-SUn,-CTP-and-Manufacturing-Industry	5k	4/6/93	1	sunsite.unc.edu
47.10-SUn,-CTP-and-Manufacturing-Industry.gz	3k	5/26/94	5	ftp.fcu.edu.tw
47.10-SUn,-CTP-and-Manufacturing-Industry.Z	3k	4/6/93	5	solomon.technet.sg
arc-100-150-manufacturing-kits	4k	7/27/93	1	sunsite.unc.edu
clari.biz.industry.manufacturing.Z	1k	4/19/94	5	unix.hensa.ac.uk
Hy-Tek_Manufacturing.Z	1k	11/29/92	2	snowhite.cis.uoguelph.ca
manufacturing	-	7/14/94	1	linc.cis.upenn.edu
manufacturing.asc	1k	4/12/94	1	sunsite.unc.edu
manufacturing.fall93	3k	11/30/93	1	pencil.cs.missouri.edu
manufacturing.how.to.book.the.film	3k	11/30/93	1	pencil.cs.missouri.edu
manufacturing.html	1k	7/14/94	1	linc.cis.upenn.edu
manufacturing.playdates.old	3k	11/30/93	1	pencil.cs.missouri.edu
manufacturing.review.insight	6k	11/30/93	1	pencil.cs.missouri.edu
manufacturing.review.nation	12k	11/30/93	1	pencil.cs.missouri.edu
manufacturing.review.short	5k	11/30/93	1	pencil.cs.missouri.edu
MANUFACTURING_CONSENT.2022	4k	7/27/93	5	unix.hensa.ac.uk
Motherboard-manufacturing	6k	7/9/93	1	sunsite.unc.edu
NEC-Vr4400-and-ARC-manufacturing-kits	23k	7/21/93	1	sunsite.unc.edu
sci.engr.manufacturing	-	6/21/94	2	cs.dal.ca
sci.engr.manufacturing	30k	6/7/93	5	unix.hensa.ac.uk
sci.engr.manufacturing	-	6/22/94	5	athene.uni-paderborn.de
sci.engr.manufacturing.Z	2k	8/19/94	5	unix.hensa.ac.uk

▶ *These are some of the files found by Archie when searching for the word "manufacturing."*

Name	Size	Date	Zone	Host
guitar-tuner.hqx	75k	11/19/93	5	solomon.technet.sg
guitar.and.other.machines	3k	7/5/93	1	cs.uwp.edu
guitar.catalogs	3k	1/7/93	1	unixd1.cis.pitt.edu
guitar.ep	3k	4/3/94	1	cs.uwp.edu
Guitar.faq	36k	8/23/94	1	cs.uwp.edu
Guitar.faq	-	7/23/94	1	cs.uwp.edu
Guitar.faq	-	8/27/94	1	cs.uwp.edu
Guitar.faq	35k	7/31/94	5	athene.uni-paderborn.de
Guitar.faq	-	8/10/94	5	athene.uni-paderborn.de
Guitar.faq	-	8/10/94	5	athene.uni-paderborn.de
Guitar.faq	-	7/26/94	5	unix.hensa.ac.uk
Guitar.faq.Z	17k	8/23/94	5	unix.hensa.ac.uk
guitar.gif	1k	1/5/93	1	ee.lbl.gov
guitar.gif	76k	10/24/93	1	cs.uwp.edu
guitar.html.gz	8k	6/9/94	5	athene.uni-paderborn.de
guitar.html.Z	11k	6/9/94	1	cs.uwp.edu
guitar.html.Z	11k	6/9/94	5	unix.hensa.ac.uk
guitar.mag.alex.Z	10k	8/26/91	1	syrinx.umd.edu
guitar.noir	5k	5/23/93	1	cs.uwp.edu
guitar.noir	6k	6/1/93	5	faramir.informatik.uni-oldenburg.de
guitar.noir.gif	229k	6/17/93	5	faramir.informatik.uni-oldenburg.de
guitar.noir.inner.gif	70k	6/8/93	1	cs.uwp.edu
guitar.noir.inner.gif	70k	6/17/93	5	faramir.informatik.uni-oldenburg.de
guitar.prac.mus.84	12k	6/8/93	5	faramir.informatik.uni-oldenburg.de
guitar.prac.mus.93	4k	6/8/93	5	faramir.informatik.uni-oldenburg.de
guitar.readme	-	5/24/94	5	ftp.luth.se
guitar.refinish	13k	3/16/94	1	unixd1.cis.pitt.edu
guitar.refinish	13k	3/16/94	1	unixd1.cis.pitt.edu
Guitar.tab.editor.or.gz	1k	1/28/94	5	lth.se

▶ *Many of the files available by anonymous FTP are not business related, so you can find lots of interesting things about hobbies and other interests.*

World Wide Web (WWW) An Internet service that allows users to retrieve hypertext and graphics from various sites. Often called simply "the Web," this has become one of the most popular Internet services in the past two years. In fact, many Internet information providers are only publishing using the Web.

WWW Virtual Library

Because the type of information on the World Wide Web is so different from that in Gopherspace, it is much more difficult to index. However, because it is so much easier to see the information in context on the Web than on a Gopher server, a well-organized Web page can take you where you want to go faster.

With that in mind, the best place to start when you are looking for information on the Web is the *WWW Virtual Library*. It is a list of broad subjects, each of which is maintained by an expert in the field, so that you can quickly narrow your search. There are dozens of topics, and more are added each month. Under each heading are long lists of related Web servers (and some Gopher and FTP sites) that relate to the given subject.

The sections in the Virtual Library are maintained by volunteers who know a great deal concerning what is available on the World Wide Web and in Gopherspace about a particular topic. However, no one can know everything, particularly because many new servers appear with little notice. Thus, the maintainers of the Virtual Library rely on readers to help keep their sections as complete as possible. Every Virtual Library page has the mail addresses of the maintainers, who are very open to suggestions for additional listings for their sections. In this way, the people on the Web itself help make the Virtual Library as complete as possible.

You may remember the discussion about *hypertext* — text or pictures that are linked to other documents — from the World Wide Web section earlier in this book. After you've searched for what you want by way of the WWW Virtual Library, you choose a starting point from a Virtual Library menu to get to a home page. From that page, you can start browsing; this is a hypertext link.

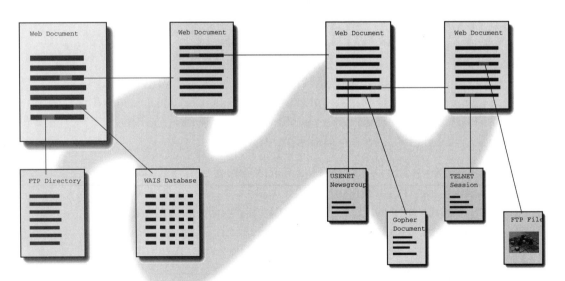

▶ *This illustration shows how hypertext works.*

Web Crawlers

Gopherspace has one search mechanism: Veronica. The World Wide Web has many different search programs, none of which are terribly complete or all that easy to use. These programs are often called *Web crawlers* or *spiders*, possibly taking the web metaphor a bit too far.

Using a Web crawler is like using Veronica: you specify the word or words you want to use for your search, and the program returns all of what it thinks of as relevant links. Many different programs act as Web crawlers, and the ways in which they process the words you search for and how they list their output is quite different.

You can see why a program that indexes the Web would have a hard time when you think about how the information is presented. On some Web pages, the most important words are those in the regular text; on others, the most important words are in headings on the page; in others, it is in the links themselves. Unless you index all of these things, you will probably miss some important information and your index database will be incomplete.

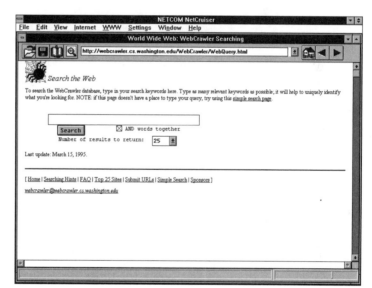

▶ *This is how some Web crawlers prompt for the item you want to search for. Note that you can enter more than one word and the Web crawler will search for items that include all of the words.*

▶ *This is the result of searching for "pond plants." As you can see, some of the resulting links probably have nothing to do with ponds, but the page they refer to have both words in it.*

Searching for Internet Users

Because the Internet is so spread out and has no centralized support system, finding Internet users can be quite difficult. Searching for information on the Internet by itself is difficult, but at least there are many indexes and catalogs arranged by subject. Finding a person can be next to impossible unless you have some idea where they might have their Internet account, and even then you might have no luck.

The Internet is very different from the phone system. If you want someone's phone number and you know what city they live in, you can call directory information in that city and ask. However, even this is not foolproof: they may not have a phone or they may not be listed at the phone number in their house (such as a child or a temporary resident). Of course, if you don't know what city they live in, you are also out of luck. You can't call information and say "I think she works for a company in New York City" and expect to get a number for that person.

Because there are no "cities" on the Internet, you can't even find a starting place to look. You might know what company someone works for, but few companies have central mail address directories, even if you could figure out which host to connect to. If the person in question works for a university, you may be in luck, because universities are the most likely Internet sites to have such directories. However, that only accounts for a tiny fraction of the people on the Internet.

Electronic Frontier Foundation (EFF) A large, nonprofit organization concerned with Internet-related privacy and access issues. The EFF educates and lobbies extensively in Washington, D.C., and often teaches local law enforcement agencies how computer technology is and is not like other things with which they are familiar. The EFF is one of the strongest supporters of personal freedoms on the Internet.

Security Concerns

Security and privacy concerns have also made searching for people on the Internet more difficult. Few network administrators want programs poking around their networks looking to see if a particular person has a login on one of their machines. Thus, many sites do not support searching with the finger command. This has also stymied the next main method of searching, the Netfind program, which also heavily relies on finger.

Recently, there has been a movement to make searching for users easier, although the results have not been terribly encouraging. Some printed white-pages listings for the Internet are available, such as the NetPages from Aldea, but they contain addresses for only a fraction of people on the Internet. Because no method for contacting everyone on the Internet exists, telling everyone how to get listed in the electronic or paper listings is impossible.

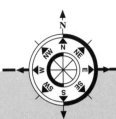

PEM (Privacy Enhanced Mail) An encryption standard commonly used to secure Internet mail. PEM lets only the desired recipient read your messages. It also lets you authenticate your mail, which means that the person who receives it can be assured that you were the person who sent the mail.

Of course, online user directories are being planned, but these may fail pretty badly as well. Even the "official" registry, supported by an NSF grant, is woefully small and difficult to get listed in. Few Internet host systems encourage their users to be listed in these directories, so most users don't even know that such directories exist. Private services — such as CompuServe and America Online — have excellent directories with good search tools; the Internet doesn't.

When All Else Fails...

Probably the best way to find someone's Internet mail address is to call them on the telephone and ask. It is still much easier to track down someone's phone number than their Internet address. This is particularly true these days when someone might have three or four different Internet mail addresses, but only read the mail from one of them regularly; you would not want to send your initial message to an account they never look at.

PART 6

Future of the Internet

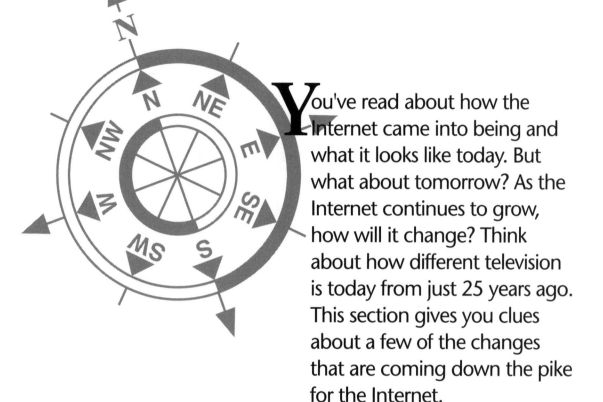

You've read about how the Internet came into being and what it looks like today. But what about tomorrow? As the Internet continues to grow, how will it change? Think about how different television is today from just 25 years ago. This section gives you clues about a few of the changes that are coming down the pike for the Internet.

Universal Internet Mail

Because mail is one of the most popular uses of the Internet, it will probably be one of the Internet features that will be enhanced the quickest. Internet mail has a major advantage over other Internet features in that almost everyone, no matter how computerphobic they are, can understand mail because it is so much like regular mail. If you think about the variety of things that appear in your postal mailbox, you get a feeling for what the future of Internet mail might be.

encryption Scrambling a message so that it is virtually impossible for someone else to read the message unless they have a key. You use encryption to maintain privacy when sending messages, and also to verify the identity of the sender of a message. Many different types of encryption are used on the Internet, and none of them are compatible with each other.

MIME The standard for enclosing binary files in Internet mail, MIME stands for *Multipurpose Internet Mail Extensions*; it allows you to specify the type of attachment you are making to your Internet mail. Many nonmail programs, such as the World Wide Web, also use the MIME standard to make it easier for client programs to read files.

Sending Binary Files

One of the first enhancements that needs to be made is the ability to send binary files along with regular Internet mail. *MIME*, a standard for binary mail, has been around for years; many mail clients do not support it, though, or support it in a way that is difficult to use. Further, many local networks connected to the Internet don't support MIME-enhanced mail.

Binary attachments are important because they let you attach almost anything to a piece of mail. For example, you can send voice recordings and pictures as part of your Internet mail. This makes Internet mail work very similarly to voice mail and fax systems, both of which have become a standard part of almost every office in the United States. Binary attachments also let you pass fully formatted documents, and even videos, as easily as jotting a quick note.

Problems with Binary Attachments

The biggest problem with binary attachments is file size. A short movie or a long voice-mail message can take up a megabyte of disk space. While a message like this takes almost no time at all to pass over most of the Internet, it takes about 15 minutes to get to your computer over a standard modem. Few people want to wait that long just to get a short message.

Another important aspect of universal Internet mail is the ability for every computer system to exchange mail with every other system. Again, the standards for this have been in place for many years, and many products let non-Internet systems trade mail with Internet hosts. However, many companies still have not upgraded, and thus, have no access to millions of Internet users who regularly use mail.

Merging with Entertainment and Telephone Networks

Until now, most home and small office computers have connected to the Internet through standard telephone lines via modems. While this connectivity method is acceptable for some uses, even the fastest modems are too slow for many of the things people envision for the future of the Internet, such as video and film. We'll need much faster connections at a reasonable cost.

Fortunately, most people will have access to such connections in the next five to ten years. Cable television systems and telephone companies are almost ready to start wiring homes and offices for high-speed connections in large numbers. Most of these companies have begun testing such systems, and the initial results look promising.

Roadblocks to Access

This is not to say that everyone will have this kind of access soon. First and foremost, the many companies that might provide this kind of high-speed communications want to eliminate their competition from the market, and are spending lots of money lobbying Congress and the public in attempts to accomplish this. At the same time, these companies are looking at merging with some competitors to get around the same regulations they seek.

America Online A large bulletin board system with over 1 million users. America Online, also called "AOL," was the first of the big three BBSs — Prodigy, America Online, and CompuServe — to have more than just a mail connection to the Internet. It introduced both a Gopher client and a Usenet news client in spring of 1994.

CompuServe Probably the best-known bulletin board system with over 2 million users. CompuServe was one of the earliest of the large systems not directly connected to the Internet to offer Internet mail access to its users. Recently, CompuServe has embraced the Internet by giving its users access to features such as Usenet news.

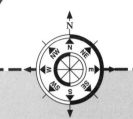

MUD A program that simulates a place where you can move around, talk to other users, and interact with your surroundings. MUD stands for Multi-User Dimensions or Multi-User Dungeons (depending on whom you ask), and most are centered on fantasy themes, such as dragons and science fiction. Many Internet MUDs even let you create parts of the environment for others to use.

Of course, technical difficulties might make the service too expensive for many homes or offices. For example, cable television companies would have to add an incredible amount of new hardware in every neighborhood in order to modify the current cable system to allow home use of the Internet. Although phone companies would need to change less, they still have to change a great deal, and those costs would most certainly be added to your phone bills.

Interactive Entertainment

With high-speed connections, the Internet can offer many more services than it does now. Most of today's interactive services — such as Gopher and the World Wide Web — are good for information gathering and socializing, but let's face it: they aren't much fun. The future of the Internet could be driven by new forms of entertainment that are currently unimaginable.

Where We Are Now

For example, many multiplayer games can be played over modems or over the Internet currently. The most common type of multiplayer games are battle games where players form teams or just fight for themselves, but there are also many nonviolent games as well. Such games might proliferate and become the main choice for many game players in the future.

For example, imagine a sports network where teams of people compete in games such as soccer and basketball over the Internet. Your skills on offense and defense are combined with other random factors to help your team, but the best teams would probably be the ones with the best cooperation. It would certainly be an interesting challenge to work with people whom you have never met face to face.

Where We're Going

The future Internet also opens up to kinds of entertainment that few people have ever thought of before. "Virtual coffeehouses," where people chat, already exist. Imagine such a place if everyone looked and spoke as they would if they were really in the same room. Such an environment would let you meet and interact with people in a way you can't today.

Other forms of entertainment certainly will also spring up. Social activities that require people to travel might be replaced by virtual communities, such as bridge tournaments, political rallies, and so on. Of course, sex-as-entertainment sells almost everywhere, and many people have already started to stake out some of that territory on the Internet today. Dozens of other types of entertainment could become common, assuming that they don't cost much and are more interesting than the forms of entertainment we currently enjoy.

NII

The *National Information Infrastructure*, better known as the NII, is a proposal by the U.S. government to help integrate all digital communications that are related to information throughout the country. The government's aim is to help make digital information more easily accessible to everyone: schools, businesses, community groups, individuals, and so on. Like any major government initiative, the NII has many supporters and many detractors.

Implications for the Future

Depending on how the NII is implemented, it could make a huge difference in the way that Americans get information in the next decade. For example, if the initiative demands that everyone get a particular level of access, that could make the system more open.

On the other hand, if the initiative specifies only how information transporters must support the digital network, many people could have little or no access.

The NII also brings up many issues central to the Internet today, such as how much government support there should be for the communications backbone, and how much control commercial vendors should have on the content. As has been shown in many other fields, after the government has a certain level of involvement in a system, it may never take its hand out. These arguments will go on for decades, as they already have on a smaller scale on the Internet over the past 25 years.

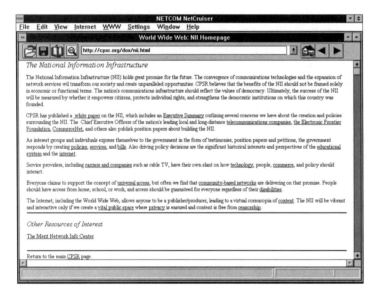

▶ There are many public interest groups debating the NII. Some of these groups, like the Computer Professionals for Social Responsibility, have a great deal of information about the NII available on the Internet. As Congress moves forward with the various NII proposals, these groups post the various working papers and comments about them.

Lobbying for the NII

Many groups will lobby Congress for different parts of the NII legislation. For example, the Electronic Frontier Foundation (EFF) has already begun helping write legislation to ensure that the principles of free speech embodied in the First Amendment of the U.S. Constitution are fully embodied in the NII. Some other important publicly minded groups, such as operators of Free-nets, are also lobbying, but on a more local level. Of course, commercial groups such as the CIX and the individual phone companies and cable operators are also lobbying hard for the greatest profit for their companies.

Can the NII Keep Pace?

Because the NII is a government initiative, it is moving much more slowly than the commercial changes on the Internet and the other systems covered by the NII. By the time the various lobbyists and others in Washington get to some agreement about what the NII should look like, the Internet may look so different that they will have to scrap the NII and start over. Alternatively, some large companies may wait to invest in Internet-related technologies until they have a better idea about how the NII will change the current structure.

It is certainly unclear what the NII will mean to the average Internet user. Many people think that the NII will pretty much bypass the Internet and be related mostly to television and telephones; in this case, the Internet will probably continue to grow, but not become much more important. On the other hand, the NII could mandate that the phone and cable TV companies make the Internet the main method of transferring data to the home. In this case, Internet users could be in for a wild ride, because that kind of growth of data might make it hard for today's type of Internet messages to get through. However, such a change would also mean that the kind of Internet information, and the way you get it, will be very different in the next decade.

Free-nets Bulletin board systems connected to the Internet that users access for free or a nominal fee. The idea is to give all the people in a community free access to computing and the Internet. Volunteer staff and local donations usually support Free-nets.

NII (National Information Infrastructure) A broad proposal for the U.S. government to set up standards and governing bodies for the transmission of digital data. The NII is still under debate, and the final content may be affected more by corporate lobbyists than by citizens because of the significant impact the NII will have on how private networks can operate.

Growth Statistics

As you have seen, it is impossible to determine how fast the Internet is growing because it is impossible to count the number of Internet users. However, people love numbers, and therefore, many sets of numbers that purport to show how fast the Internet is growing are tossed around. When you see such numbers, you should certainly view them with a fair amount of healthy skepticism.

An Indisputable Conclusion

Regardless of our inability to make accurate counts, it is very clear that both the number of people and the amount of information on the Internet are growing rapidly. Many of the companies that sell Internet accounts to individuals are having an enviable (but real) problem of growing too rapidly. The list of commercial Internet sites grows every week, as does the list of interesting Gopher and World Wide Web information servers.

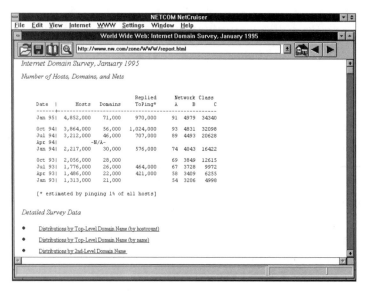

▶ *The number of host computers is often used to chart the growth of the Internet.*

One of the numbers most used by people wanting to chart the growth of the Internet is the number of host computers. This number is only somewhat countable because many networks don't reveal how many hosts are on their networks. Also, the way that many people then determine how many people are on the Internet is quite questionable because they assume a fixed number of people per host, and they also assume that the number doesn't change over time.

The future growth of the Internet will be even harder to gauge because more and more people will have only partial access to the Internet. It is likely that as new information services spring up, they will first allow only electronic mail or maybe World Wide Web access, but not give access to all Internet services. These companies may expand what they offer, but only in response to customer demand.

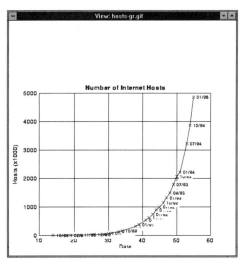

▶ *An impressive, if not terribly useful, chart of the increase in the estimated number of Internet hosts over time.*

Growth Outside the U.S.

Much of this book discusses the Internet in relation to how it operates in the United States. This is because a great deal of the best information available about the Internet is based in the U.S., and because so many of the people using the Internet's advanced resources are in the U.S. However, ignoring the rest of the world's impact on the Internet is unrealistic.

Varying Levels of Connectivity

The Internet's growth in other countries may not be as rapid as the growth in the United States, but it is still quite significant. In some countries, particularly in Europe, universities and large corporations are networked as well as they are in the United States, and most of these places are connected to the Internet. In other countries, only a handful of sites have any Internet connectivity, but those sites are very important to the countries and are working hard to expand their Internet presence.

Country	Number of hosts
United Kingdom	155,706
Germany	149,193
Canada	127,516
Australia	127,514
Japan	72,409
France	71,899
Netherlands	59,729
Sweden	53,294
Finland	49,598
Switzerland	47,401
Norway	38,759
Italy	23,616
Spain	21,147
Austria	20,130

▶ *This chart shows the countries with the most hosts (estimated) from a recent survey of the international Internet.*

It's impossible to generalize about which kind of countries are doing what on the Internet. For example, tiny Finland has one of the most active Internet presences in all of Europe. Some countries are adding Internet connectivity cautiously while their immediate neighbors are spending much of their computing budgets on better Internet connections.

Country	Host growth
Argentina	8,167%
Ukraine	994%
Cyprus	660%
Romania	466%
Thailand	334%
Tunisia	318%
Bulgaria	276%
Greece	249%
Malaysia	204%
Denmark	175%
Chile	170%
Czech Rep.	169%
New Zealand	157%
Costa Rica	153%
Latvia	150%
Belgium	147%
Russian Fed. (SU)	142%
Turkey	140%
India	129%
Hungary	122%
France	117%
Kuwait	115%
Ireland	103%

▶ This chart shows the countries with the greatest six-month growth rate of hosts (estimated) from a recent survey of the international Internet. Note that these numbers are not terribly accurate because some countries weren't counted and others counted hosts differently between the two surveys. You can see, however, that the list is dominated by smaller countries.

Implications of More International Access

Of course, the numbers don't say everything. Imagine how having a much better connection to the rest of the world could affect many of the small countries of the world. Many people hope that such connections will help better the standard of living in those countries. Other people, particularly those living within those countries, worry that the outside influences could devastate the culture of their countries. They point to how American entertainment has pushed out local entertainment in many countries, and how American politics would easily follow new Internet connections. Still, the number of Internet sites, even in the most impoverished countries, continues to grow unabated and will certainly challenge the way that those countries communicate with the rest of the world.

Security in the Future

Because the Internet is so decentralized, it is not at all secure relative to the security found with other networks. It is unlikely that the Internet will become much more secure in the near future, although many people are working hard to add security features to the Internet. Note that many networks commonly used in offices are just as insecure as the Internet, so you should probably not view Internet security as worse than that of the typical system.

Security Problems

The major security problems of the Internet fall into two broad categories: *authentication* and *privacy*. Authentication is the ability to prove who you are and to have some assurance that a person or system with whom you are communicating is who they say they are. To many people, privacy is more important than authentication: you want to be sure that no one other than the recipient can read the mail you are sending.

To make the Internet better for commercial consumer transactions, such as ordering merchandise through the World Wide Web or Internet mail, many companies are setting up systems that will allow you to pay with electronic money. Because of the lack of authentication and privacy, the typical way you would pay for something — by credit card — is too risky on the Internet. Someone could find your credit card number by watching your mail or transactions, and then use that information to pretend to be you and order merchandise on your card.

Many civil libertarians are quite concerned about privacy, particularly privacy from government spying. Because messages on the Internet can be sent on almost any route without you knowing the route, it is not difficult for someone (inside or outside the government) to scan all the information going through certain key points on the Internet. In fact, many long-time Internet users are more worried about government spying than they are about *crackers*.

One Solution

The answer to privacy concerns is *encryption*, the method for making messages unreadable by anyone other than the recipient. Many types of encryption have been available for years, but no single standard has been widely implemented on the Internet. Many companies are supporting a standard called *privacy-enhanced mail (PEM)*, although few mail client programs today support PEM very well.

CERT (Computer Emergency Response Team) A security force for the Internet. CERT is a clearinghouse of information about network security, known security problems on the Internet, and attempted (or successful) break-ins. CERT has an FTP site that has definitive versions of common Internet server software.

cracker Someone who — just for the challenge — tries to thwart computer security systems by gaining access to the systems. Sometimes this activity exposes flaws in system security, which may be beneficial, but many states have laws against accessing a computer that isn't your own without permission.

Electronic Frontier Foundation (EFF)
One of the first large groups concerned with Internet-related privacy and access issues. The EFF does extensive education and lobbying in Washington D.C., and often educates local law enforcement agencies about how computer technology is and is not like other things they are familiar with. The EFF has some of the strongest supporters of personal freedoms on the Internet.

Encryption comes at a cost, however. Everyone must remember even more passwords and personal identification numbers than they do now to be able to use encryption. Also, many companies on the Internet are using different methods for encryption, which forces you to deal with different encryption programs for each Internet service you use. This may all be resolved in the next five years, but it also might get worse as companies dig in their heels about not using other people's security mechanisms.

Issues for the Future

As the Internet expands in the United States and around the world, security issues will become much more important. Countries will have different laws regarding what can and cannot be encrypted, and what methods can be used. The globalization of the Internet will have a profound effect on how we view our communications and how countries interact with each other.

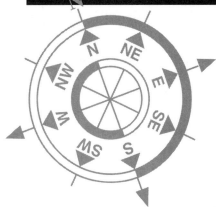

INTERNET PROVIDERS

This list, adapted from one developed at the InterNIC, is a fraction of the hundreds (or maybe thousands-of companies through which you can get an Internet connection. Remember, pricing for Internet connections varies widely; it's a good idea to shop around to get exactly what you want, at the best price. The phone numbers listed are voice numbers for you to call and ask questions; don't call on your modem!

Access InfoSystems
Phone: 707-422-1034
Area Codes: 707, 510

ACM Network Services
Phone: 817-776-6876
Area Codes: 800, 817, nationwide

Aimnet Information Services
Phone: 408-257-0900
Area Codes: 408, 415

AlterNet (UUNET Technologies)
Phone: 800-4UUNET4
Area Codes: All

American Information Systems, Inc. (AIS)
Phone: 708-413-8400
Area Codes: 708, 312, 800

APK Public Access UNI*
Phone: 216-481-9428
Area Code: 216

ANS
Phone: 800-456-8267, 703-758-7700
Area Codes: Nationwide

BARRNet
Phone: 415-725-1790

Beckemeyer Development (BDT)
Phone: 510-530-9637

The Black Box ·
Phone: 713-480-2684
Area Code: 713

Blythe Systems
Phone: 212-348-2875
Area Codes: 212, 718

California Online!
Phone: 707-586-3060
Area Codes: 415, 510, 707, 408, 916, 209

CAPCON Library Network
Phone: 202-331-5771
Area Codes: 202, 301, 410, 703

CCnet Communications
Phone: 510-988-0680
Area Codes: 510, 415, 408

CENTURION Technology, Inc.
Phone: 813-572-5556
Area Codes: 800, 813

CERFNET
Phone: 800-876-2373, 619-455-3900
Area Codes: 800, 310, 415, 510, 619, 714, 818

CICnet
Phone: 800-947-4754, 313-998-6703

Cloud 9 Internet
Phone: 914-682-0626
Area Code: 914

Colorado SuperNet, Inc.
Phone: 303-296-8202
Area Codes: 303, 719, 800

CONCERT
Phone: 919-248-1999

The Connection
Phone: 201-435-4414

Connix: The Connecticut Internet Exchange
Phone: 203-349-7059
Area Code: 203

Creative Data Consultants (silly.com)
Phone: 718-229-0489 x23
Area Codes: 718, 212, 516

CRL Network Services
Phone: 415-837-5300
Area Codes: 210, 212, 213, 214, 310, 404, 415, 510, 512, 602, 617

CSUnet (California State Unversity)
Phone: 310-985-9445
Area Codes: All in California

CTS Network Services
Phone: 619-637-3637
Area Code: 619

CyberGate, Inc.
Phone: 305-428-4283
Area Codes: 305, 407, 813, 904

Cyberlink Communications
Phone: 206-281-5397, 515-945-7000
Area Code: 206

Dallas Vietnamese Network
Phone: 214-248-8701
Area Code: 214

DELPHI Internet Services Corp
Phone: 800-695-4005
Area Codes: All - 617 direct, others through Sprintnet and Tymnet

DFW Internet Services, Inc.
Phone: 817-332-5116
Area Codes: 214, 817

DigiLink Network Services
Phone: 310-542-7421

Digital Express Group
Phone: 301-220-2020, 410-813-2724,
800-969-9090
Area Codes: 201, 202, 301, 410, 609, 703,
718, 908

The Dorsai Embassy
Phone: 718-392-3667
Area Codes: 718, 212, 201, 203, 914, 516

The Duck Pond Public Unix
Area Code: 408

Earthlink Network, Inc.
Phone: 213-644-9500
Area Codes: 213, 310, 818

Echo Communications Group
Phone: 212-255-3839
Area Codes: 201, 516

The Eden Matrix
Phone: 512-478-9900
Area Code: 512

The Edge
Phone: 615-455-9915 (Tullahoma),
(615-726-8700 (Nashville)
Area Code: 615

EriNet Online Communications
Phone: 513-436-1700
Area Code: 513

Escape (Kazan Corp.)
Phone: 212-888-8780
Area Codes: 212, 718

Eskimo North
Phone: 206-367-7457
Area Code: 206

ESNET Communications
Phone: 619-287-5943
Area Code: 619

Evergreen Internet
Phone: 602-230-9330
Area Codes: 602, 702, 801

Exchange Network Services, Inc.
Phone: 216-261-4594
Area Code: 216

FishNet (Prometheus Information Corp.)
Phone: 610-337-9994
Area Code: 610

Florida Online
Phone: 407-635-8888
Area Codes: 407, 305, 904, 813

Freelance Systems Programming
Phone: 513-254-7246
Area Code: 513

free.i.net
Phone: 503-233-4774

FullFeed Communications
Phone: 608-246-4239
Area Codes: 608, 414, 715

FXnet
Phone: 704-338-4670
Area Codes: 800, 704, 803

Genuine Computing Resources
Global Connect Inc
Phone: 804-229-4484
Area Codes: 804, 800

Global Enterprise Services, Inc.
Phone: 609-897-7324, 800-35-TIGER

Hevanet Communications
Phone: 503-228-3520
Area Code: 503

HoloNet/Information Access Technologies, Inc.
Phone: 510-704-0160
Area Codes: Nationwide

IACNet
Phone: 513-887-8877

ICNet/Innovative Concepts
Phone: 313-998-0090

IDS World Network
Phone: 800-IDS-1680
Area Codes: 401, 305, 407, 914

IgLou Internet Services
Phone: 800-436-IGLOU
Area Codes: 502, 812, 606, 513

Innovative Data Services
Phone: 810-478-3554
Area Code: 810

INS Info Services
Phone: 800-546-6587
Area Codes: 800, 319, 402, 515, 712

Institute for Global Communications
Phone: 415-442-0220

INTAC Access Corporation
Phone: 201-944-1417

InterAccess Company
Phone: 800-967-1580
Area Codes: 708, 312, 815

The Internet Access Company
Phone: 617-276-7200
Area Codes: 617, 508

Internet Access Online Communications Service
Phone: 513-887-8877
Area Code: 513

Internet Atlanta
Phone: 404-410-9000
Area Codes: 404, 705, 912 (dialup); frame relay and T1 (nationwide)

Internet Express
Phone: 800-592-1240
Area Codes: 719, 303, 505, 602, 800

Internet On-Ramp, Inc
Phone: 509-927-RAMP (7267), 509-927-7267
Area Code: 509

Internetworks
Phone: 503-233-4774

InterNex Information Services, Inc.
Phone: 415-473-3060
Area Codes: 415, 408, 510

Interpath
Phone: 919-890-6305, 800-849-6305
Area Codes: 919, 800

Interport Communications Corp.
Phone: 212-989-1128
Area Codes: 212, 718

IQuest Network Services
Phone: 317-259-5050, 800-844-UNIX
Area Code: 317

KAIWAN Corporation
Phone: 714-638-2139
Area Codes: 714, 213, 310, 818, 909, 805

LI Net, Inc.
Phone: 516-476-1168
Area Code: 516

Lightside, Inc.
Phone: 818-858-9261
Area Codes: 818, 310, 714, 909

LineX Communications
Phone: 415-455-1650
Area Code: 415

Los Nettos
Phone: 310-822-1551

Long Island Information, Inc
Phone: 516-248-5381
Area Code: 516

Lyceum
Phone: 404-377-7575

Maestro Technologies, Inc.
Phone: 212-240-9600
Area Codes: 212, 718, 516

maine.net, Inc.
Phone: 207-780-6381
Area Code: 207

MCSNet
Phone: 312-248-8649
Area Codes: 312, 708, 815

MHVNet
Phone: 914-229-9853, 800-998-7131
Area Code: 914

MichNet
Phone: 313-764-9430
Area Codes: 313, 616, 517, 810, 906

MIDnet
Phone: 402-472-7600

MindSpring Enterprises, Inc.
Phone: 404-888-0725
Area Code: 404

Minnesota Regional Network (MRNet)
Phone: 612-342-2570
Area Codes: 612, 507, 218

MIX Communications
Phone: 414-228-0739
Area Code: 414

Msen Inc.
Phone: 313-998-4562
Area Codes: 800, 313, 517, 616, 906

MV Communications
Phone: 603-429-2223
Area Code: 603

NEARNET
Phone: 617-873-8730

Neighborhood Internet Connection
Phone: 201-934-1445
Area Code: 201

NeoSoft, Inc.
Phone: 713-684-5969
Area Codes: 800, 713, 409, 214, 504, 314

NetAxis
Phone: 203-969-0618

Netcom On-Line Communication Services
Phone: 408-554-8649, 800-501-8649
Area Codes: 201, 206, 212, 214, 303, 310, 312, 404, 408, 415, 503

netILLINOIS
Phone: 708-866-1825

Network Access Services
Network Intensive
Phone: 800-273-5600
Area Code: 714

Network Internet Services
Phone: 516-543-0234
Area Code: 516

The Network Link, Inc.
Phone: 619-278-5943
Area Codes: 619, 317

NevadaNet
Phone: 702-784-6861
Area Code: 702

New Jersey Computer Connection
Phone: 609-896-2799
Area Code: 609

New Mexico Technet, Inc.
Phone: 505-345-6555
Area Codes: 505, 602, 303, 915, 800

New York Net
Phone: 718-776-6811
FAX: (718-217-9407)
Area Codes: 201, 203, 212, 516, 609, 718, 908, 914, 917

North Shore Access
Phone: 617-593-3110
Area Codes: 617, 508

Northcoast Internet
Phone: 707-443-8696
Area Code: 707

NorthWest CommLink
Phone: 206-336-0103
Area Code: 206

Northwest Nexus, Inc.
Phone: 206-455-3505
Area Code: 206

NorthwestNet
Phone: 206-562-3000

Nuance Network Services
Phone: 205-533-4296
Area Code: 205

NYSERNet
Phone: 614-292-8100

Nyx
Phone: 303-871-3308
Area Code: 303

OARnet
Phone: 800-627-8101, 614-728-8100
Area Codes: 614, 419, 513, 216, 800

Old Colorado City Communications
Phone: 719-528-5849
Area Code: 719

PACCOM
Phone: 808-956-3499

Pacifier Computers
Phone: 206-693-2116
Area Code: 206

Panix
Phone: 212-787-6160

Ping
Phone: 800-746-4635, 404-399-1670
Area Codes: 404, 800 (includes Hawaii
and Alaska)

The Pipeline Network
Phone: 212-267-3636
Area Codes: Nationwide

Pioneer Global
Phone: 617-375-0200
Area Code: 617

Planet Access Networks
Phone: 201-691-4704
Area Codes: 201, 908, 319, 205

Portal Information Network
Phone: 800-433-6444, 408-973-9111
Area Codes: Nationwide

PREPnet
Phone: 412-268-7870

Primenet
Phone: 602-870-1010 ext.109
Area Code: 602

PSCNET
Phone: 412-268-4960

PSINet
Phone: 800-82PSI82, 703-620-6651

QuakeNet
Phone: 415-655-6607
Area Code: 415

The Rabbit Network, Inc.
Phone: 800-456-0094
Area Codes: 810, 800 (entire U.S. and Canada)

Real/Time Communications
Phone: 512-451-0046
Area Code: 512

Red River Net
Phone: 701-232-2227
Area Codes: 701, 218

Rocky Mountain Internet, Inc.
Phone: 800-900-RMII
Area Codes: 303, 719

SatelNET Communications
Phone: 305-434-8738
Area Code: 305

Savvy
Phone: 516-626-2090

Schunix
Phone: 508-853-0258
Area Code: 508

Scruz-Net
Phone: 800-319-5555, 408-457-5050
Area Codes: 408, 415

SeaNet
Phone: 206-343-7828

Sesquinet
Phone: 713-527-4988

Sibylline, Inc.
Phone: 501-521-4660
Area Code: 501

SIMS, Inc.
Phone: 803-762-4956
Area Code: 803

Skagit On-Line Services
Phone: 206-755-0190
Area Code: 206

South Coast Computing Services, Inc.
Phone: 800-221-6478
Area Codes: 800, 713, 918

South Valley Internet
Phone: 408-683-4533
Area Code: 408

SprintLink
Phone: 703-904-2156

SSNet, Inc.
Phone: 302-378-1386
Area Codes: 610, 302

StarNet Communications, Inc. (Winternet)
Phone: 612-941-9177
Area Code: 612

SURAnet
Phone: 301-982-4600

Synergy Communcations
Phone: 402-346-4638

SymNet
Phone: 904-385-1061
Area Code: 904

Teleport, Inc.
Phone: 503-223-4245
Area Codes: 503, 206

Telerama Public Access Internet
Phone: 412-481-3505
Area Codes: 412, 814

Tezcatlipoca, Inc.
Phone: 312-850-0181
Area Codes: 312, 708

THEnet
Phone: 512-471-2444

Townsend Communcations, Inc.
Phone: 206-385-0464
Area Code: 206

Tyrell Corp
Phone: 800-TYRELL-1
Area Codes: 816, 913, 504, 316

TZ-Link
Phone: 914-353-5443
Area Code: 914

UltraNet Communications, Inc.
Phone: 508-229-8400, 800-763-8111
Area Code: 508

US Net, Inc.
Phone: 301-572-5926
Area Codes: 301, 202, 703

UUnet Technologies
Please see AlterNet

VERnet
Phone: 804-924-0616

ViaNet Communications
Phone: 415-903-2242
Area Codes: 408, 415, 213, 818, 310

Vnet Internet Access, Inc.
Phone: 800-377-3282
Area Codes: 704, 910, 919

WestNet
Phone: 914-967-7816
Area Code: 914

Widomaker Communications
Phone: 804-253-7621
Area Code: 804

WiscNet
Phone: 608-262-8874

@wizard.com
Phone: 702-871-4461
Area Code: 702

Wizvax Communications
Phone: 518-271-6005
Area Code: 518

WLN
Phone: 800-DIAL-WLN, 800-342-5956,
206-923-4000
Area Codes: 800, 206, 509, 503, 208, 406,
360

WorldWide Access
Phone: 708-367-1870
Area Codes: 312, 708, 815, 414

WVnet
Phone: 304-293-5192

XMission
Phone: 801-539-0852
Area Code: 801

Zilker Internet Park
Phone: 512-206-3850
Area Code: 512

Zocalo Engineering
Phone: 510-540-8000
Area Codes: 510, 415

GLOSSARY

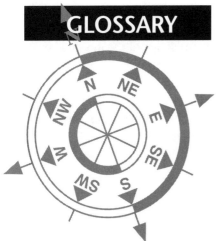

America Online A large bulletin board system with more than one million users. America Online, also called "AOL," was the first of the "big three" BBSs (Prodigy, America Online, CompuServe) to have more than just a mail connection to the Internet. AOL introduced both a Gopher client and a Usenet news client in spring of 1994.

anonymous FTP The use of the FTP program to connect to a host computer on the Internet, access its public directories, and transfer files from the host to your computer. Anonymous FTP is the most common way to search for and download files. Hundreds of host computers on the Internet let anyone use anonymous FTP to look through directories for files they want.

Archie (from archive) A program that lets you search a list of files that you can download from other host computers using anonymous FTP.

ARPAnet The network run by the U.S. Department of Defense Advanced Research Projects Agency that was the original backbone of the Internet. The ARPAnet was supposed to be a research network that also linked Defense Department affiliates. ARPA turned over the education-related portion of the ARPAnet to the U.S. National Science Foundation, which made it part of their NSFnet.

ASCII A set of standard characters (letters, numbers, punctuation, and control characters) used on computers. An ASCII file is a text file that almost any program can read. ASCII is the acronym for American Standard Code for Information Interchange.

authentication The process of establishing the identity of someone before permitting access to requested information or mail. Generally, authentication involves the use of a password.

BITNET (Because It's Time Network) A network of university computers that is separate from, but connected to, the Internet. BITNET is slowly fading away as the mainframe computers on which most of BITNET runs are decommissioned, but it is still a major force in academic computing. BITNET computers are not on an active network, but instead have nonpersistent connections.

bulletin board systems (BBSs) Computers that people can access through modems to use the BBS services. Some BBSs are on the Internet, although most are not. BBSs often have downloadable files, discussion areas, and other features that make them popular. You can use some BBSs for free, but others charge a monthly or hourly fee.

CERT (Computer Emergency Response Team) A security force for the Internet. CERT is a clearinghouse of information about network security, known Internet security problems, and attempted (or successful) break-ins. CERT has an FTP site that contains definitive versions of common Internet server software.

c shell A user interface for people whose Internet providers run on character-based UNIX systems. The c shell is one of the oldest, most common, user interfaces still widely used — and it shows. Unless you are a computer weenie, it is unlikely that you will like using the c shell much.

chat An old Internet multi-user discussion system. It has been replaced almost completely by Internet Relay Chat (IRC).

CIX (Commercial Internet Exchange) The first major industry group for companies who provide Internet access. Because CIX is made up of competitors in a constantly changing market, it is a somewhat volatile group. CIX also lobbies the U. S. Government on Internet-related issues.

client/server software Software that is split between a server, which performs most underlying processing, and a client, which mostly communicates with the user. The term "client/server" has become widely used in the computer industry to describe database and information retrieval systems in which the user runs a program from their personal computer that interacts with a database program on a host computer. Most of the major Internet services (such as mail, Usenet news, and the World Wide Web) use the client/server model.

client program Software that interfaces with server programs. A client program often looks different on each computer that runs it, taking on each computer's best features. Many different client programs can interact with one server program.

CNIDR (Clearinghouse for Networked Information Discovery and Retrieval) A government-funded group that supports Internet search software. CNIDR (pronounced "snyder") collects these tools and, in a few cases, maintains them.

CompuServe Probably the best-known bulletin board system with over two million users. CompuServe was one of the first large systems that is not directly connected to the Internet to offer Internet mail access to its users. Recently, CompuServe has embraced the Internet by giving its users access to features like Usenet news.

CoSN (Consortium for School Networking) A non-profit organization that organizes K-12 teachers, hardware and software vendors, and Internet providers. CoSN has taken an active role in educating teachers and parents about the Internet and how it can be used for education.

cracker Someone who — just for the challenge — tries to thwart computer security systems by gaining access to the systems. Sometimes this activity exposes flaws in system security, which may be beneficial, but many states have laws against accessing without permission a computer that isn't your own.

domain name system (DNS) The method by which Internet addresses (such as "mit.edu") are converted into computer-readable IP addresses (such as "182.156.12.24"). DNS is one of the most flexible, powerful technical features of the Internet, letting computers appear and disappear from the Internet without causing problems. DNS also makes sending messages much easier, because all names do not have to be in a central repository.

download To copy a file from a remote system to your computer, using data communication links. Downloading files from anonymous FTP servers is a popular way to get freeware and shareware.

Electronic Frontier Foundation (EFF) A large, nonprofit organization concerned with Internet-related privacy and access issues. The EFF educates and lobbies extensively in Washington, D.C., and often teaches local law enforcement agencies how computer technology is and is not like other things with which they are familiar. The EFF is one of the strongest supporters of personal freedoms on the Internet.

e-mail (electronic mail) Internet users often use the term "e-mail" to differentiate Internet messages from the postal mail that is more familiar to the rest of the world.

encryption The process of scrambling a message so that it is virtually impossible for someone to read without the key. Encryption maintains privacy when sending messages and verifies the sender's identity. The Internet uses many different kinds of encryption, and none of them are compatible with each other.

ERIC (Educational Resources Information Center) A clearinghouse of general information for teachers, funded by the U.S. Department of Education. ERIC sponsors AskERIC, an Internet site with lots of online teaching resources for K-12 teachers.

FAQ (Frequently Asked Questions) A file that answers questions that appear regularly on a Usenet newsgroup. FAQs are supposed to prevent newcomers from asking the same common questions over and over again. The term "FAQ" has

now moved beyond Usenet and is used for anything that answers the most common questions about a topic.

file A group of characters stored on a disk. Files may contain anything from text to pictures to programs to movies, and so on. Most programs refer to the file by their names.

finger A UNIX command used as an Internet service that tells you information about a user on another computer, such as when the user last logged on. Not all computers run finger servers.

flame To attack someone in a discussion, usually with language much harsher than necessary. Flames are usually personal, even when the flamer is attacking ideas. The term comes from the concept of a "heated" debate.

Free-nets Bulletin board systems connected to the Internet that users access for free or for a nominal fee. The idea behind is to give all the people in a community free access to computing and the Internet. Volunteer staff and local donations usually support Free-nets.

freeware Software that you can use and copy with no obligation. People write freeware because it makes them feel good or to hone their programming and design skills. You are not allowed to sell or alter most freeware programs, but you can give away freeware.

FTP The Internet's file transfer protocol. FTP is one of the older standards on the Internet, and most FTP client software is fairly unfriendly and difficult to use. On the other hand, FTP is an efficient way to transfer files between systems and to distribute information on request to Internet users.

FYIs (For Your Information files) A subset of Internet RFC files that provide information to Internet beginners. FYIs are often much simpler to read and cover less technical information than other RFCs.

geek A somewhat affectionate term for someone who is overly interested in computers. Similar terms of partial endearment, partial criticism include nerd, dweeb, weenie, and wonk.

GIF files Graphic images stored using the GIF bit-mapped color graphics file format. CompuServe designed the GIF format to compact images and let many kinds of computers easily display the images. The Internet has widely adopted the GIF standard.

Gopher A menu-based service that lets you easily find information on the Internet. Gopher presents all informa-tion as either a directory or a file, and most Gopher servers let you search for information as well. More than 1,000 Gopher servers are available on the Internet, and Gopher client programs exist for almost every computer.

host On the Internet, and other net-works, a host is the computer that performs centralized functions. For example, a host makes program or data files available to computers on the Internet.

HTML (HyperText Markup Language) The formatting language World Wide Web servers use. HTML documents are text files with embedded commands.

hypertext Documents that contain links to other documents. When read-ing a hypertext document, you can quickly jump to linked documents and then jump back when you feel like it. Hypertext lets you organize the infor-mation you read into different formats.

Hytelnet A program that works with telnet to let you easily browse through library catalogs. Hytelnet has a database of all known public library catalogs and information about how to navigate them when you are connected to the catalogs.

Internet Architecture Board (IAB) The group that oversees Internet technical issues. IAB oversees the IETF and the IRTF and acts as a liaison with other nontechnical Internet bodies.

Internet Engineering Task Force (IETF) The group that oversees the technical standards on which the Internet is based. The all-volunteer IETF is heaven for computer geeks. The technical decisions the IETF makes affect how the Internet functions, how fast it operates, and how well it will endure in the future.

Internet Relay Chat (IRC) A program that enables many people to talk at the same time by simply typing. Using IRC is similar to being in a conversation at a party with many people at once.

Internet Research Task Force (IRTF) The IAB's research arm, the IRTF looks at issues that will affect the Internet in the future, such as what happens after lots of growth, and how emerging technologies will affect Internet traffic.

Internet Society (ISOC) A voluntary group that acts as a focal point for building the Internet. ISOC has been particularly active in bringing non-U.S. users onto the Internet and in coordinating other Internet-related groups.

Internet Talk Radio A broadcast station that uses the Internet as its medium. Internet Talk Radio experiments with how the Internet might be used in the future for real-time data transfer and what kind of entertainment and information people on the Internet want.

IP (Internet Protocol) The standard that computers use to transmit information over the Internet. IP defines how the information will look as it travels between computers, not what the computers will do with it. IP also defines how Internet addresses work.

key In data encryption, a key is generally a sequence of characters used to encode and decode a file.

LISTSERV A program that manages mailing lists. LISTSERV has an arcane interface, but has been around for over a decade. Computers running LISTSERV still manage many important mailing lists. You can send commands to many LISTSERV mailing lists to retrieve files.

local area network (LAN) A network of computers that are all in the same place, such as an office or building. LANs have become much more common in the past few years as more companies have realized the importance of communication. Some LANs are attached to the Internet, giving each person on the LAN access to Internet resources.

lynx A character-based client program for the World Wide Web. Although lynx is not as flashy as other Web clients, such as Mosaic, it works well for the millions of Internet users who have only character-based access.

mail Messages sent over the Internet using the Simple Mail Transport Protocol (SMTP). Internet mail is by far the most popular and most used feature of the Internet. Most of the estimated 20 million people on the Internet (if there are even that many) have only mail access.

mailing list A list of users who receive copies of mail messages. When a user sends a message to the mailing list, all users in the list receive a copy. Some mailing lists reach thousands of people.

MIME (Multipurpose Internet Mail Extensions) The standard for enclosing binary files in Internet mail. MIME lets you specify the type of attachment you are making to your Internet mail. Many nonmail programs, such as the World Wide Web, also use MIME so that client programs can more easily read files.

mirror A duplicate of an FTP site. Mirrors help reduce long-haul Internet traffic by letting people download files from hosts that are closer to them. Usually, mirror sites are updated every night, so that they have the same contents as the main site.

modem A piece of hardware for connecting computers over telephone lines. Most personal computer users connect to the Internet over modems, although some have direct connections through company networks. The most common modems cost less than $100, although faster modems can cost more than $500.

Mosaic A graphical client program for the World Wide Web. To use Mosaic, you must have a direct (SLIP or PPP) connection to the Internet. Even though only a small minority of users today have a direct Internet connection, Mosaic has contributed a great deal to the Internet's recent surge in popularity.

MUD A program that simulates a place where you can move around, talk to other users, and interact with your surroundings. MUD stands for Multi-User Dimension (or Multi-User Dungeon), and most are centered on fantasy themes such as dragons and science fiction. Many Internet MUDs even let you create parts of the environment for others to use.

netiquette A play on the word "etiquette," netiquette is the proper way to behave on the Internet. This includes respecting the rights and desires of others, setting an example of how you want strangers to treat you, and acknowledging that the Internet is very different from face-to-face communication.

Netscape A graphical client program for the World Wide Web. Netscape is produced by Netscape Communications, and is available for free evaluation to anyone on the Internet. Netscape has become more popular than Mosaic among many Web users due to its greater array of features.

newsgroups Topical divisions of Usenet, a newsgroup generally has a single topic (for example, communications software for Microsoft Windows), but anyone can ask or answer questions. The term "news" is outdated: most of the discussion in newsgroups has to do with old items, not news.

NSFnet (National Science Foundation network) The network run by the National Science Foundation that was once part of ARPAnet, the Internet's original backbone. Commercial networks have supplanted most of NSFnet's usefulness.

NII (National Information Infrastructure) A broad proposal for the U.S. government to set up standards and governing bodies for digital data transmission. The NII is still under debate. Corporate lobbyists may affect NII's final content more than citizens will, because of the significant impact NII will have on how private networks can operate.

packet A group of bytes sent from one Internet host to another. Packets have variable lengths and can contain any kind of information.

PEM (Privacy Enhanced Mail) An encryption standard commonly used to secure Internet mail. PEM lets only the desired recipient read your messages. It also lets you authenticate your mail, which means that the person who receives it can be assured that you were the person who sent the mail.

point of presence (POP) A place that you dial into to get Internet access. Many Internet service companies have POPs in many cities. Usually, all of the POPs for one service provider are connected to a single set of computers.

port A number that helps TCP identify what kind of service you are asking for from another computer. Most common

Internet features — such as Gopher — have "standard port numbers" (for example, 70 for Gopher) that client software uses if you do not specify a different port number. The only time you need to know about ports is when a server requires that you use a nonstandard port number to communicate.

PPP (Point-to-Point Protocol) A fast, reliable method for connecting computers on the Internet over serial lines, such as telephone wire. PPP has become more popular than SLIP in the past few years, and many Internet service providers offer PPP connections. Using PPP or SLIP, your personal computer becomes directly connected to the Internet.

RFCs (Requests for Comments) Documents that define the Internet's technical aspects. Originally, these documents were used to get input from other technical users of the Internet before standards were defined. Many RFCs today still serve that purpose; other RFCs are simply statements of reality.

router A hardware device that connects two networks, allowing only certain traffic to pass. The Internet uses routers at almost every intersection, both to limit traffic going to smaller networks

and to help choose the most efficient way to get packets to their destination. Some routers cost less than $2,000, while others cost well over $25,000.

server In client/server network architecture, a server is a single, high-powered machine with a huge hard disk set aside to function as a file server for all the client machines in the network.

server program The program a host computer runs to communicate with users running client programs. Server programs establish a standard for communication, and all client programs must follow that standard to work properly. Many different client programs can interact with one server program.

shareware Copyrighted software that you can freely copy and try. If you like and continue to use the software, you must send the author a licensing fee.

shell A program that lets a user interact with an operating system. Programs like the MS-DOS command line and Microsoft Windows are shells to the MS-DOS operating system. Under UNIX, popular shells include the c shell and the Bourne shell.

SLIP (Serial Line IP) A fast, simple method for connecting computers on the Internet over serial lines, such as telephone wire. PPP has become more popular than SLIP in the past few years, although many Internet service providers offer SLIP connections as well as PPP connections. Using PPP or SLIP, your personal computer becomes directly connected to the Internet.

STD (Standards file) A type of RFC file that has been anointed by the IETF as an official Internet standard. STDs are the same as the RFC files; they simply have this additional designation.

TCP (Transmission Control Protocol) The Internet standard for identifying the kind of information in packets. TCP is almost always used with the IP standard, and you normally hear of them together as "TCP/IP." TCP also makes sure that data is passed with no errors.

telnet An Internet service that lets one computer act as a terminal on another computer. Using telnet, you can type on another computer as if you were directly connected to it. In this way, telnet is like common communications programs (sometimes called "terminal programs") for personal computers.

thread In a Usenet newsgroup, a chain of postings on a single subject.

UNIX A computer operating system that was originally designed at AT&T's Bell Laboratories. UNIX is the most common operating system for servers and hosts on the Internet. Almost any computer can be an Internet host, but computers running UNIX are historically the most common Internet hosts.

upload To send a file to a remote computer. A few UNIX hosts allow anyone to leave files on the computer for others to read. However, most Internet users only download files and never upload.

Usenet A widely used Internet service that organizes people's comments by topic. These topics, called newsgroups, have their own structure, with people commenting on previous comments and starting new discussions. Usenet is the second most popular Internet feature, after mail.

UUCP (UNIX-to-UNIX Copy) A common communication method for computers that are connected to the Internet only part of the time. UUCP is a very old standard that allows mail messages, Usenet news, and files, to be transferred among computers. UUCP has become less popular in recent years, although many bulletin board systems use it to pass mail.

Veronica A service that searches for files on Gopher servers. You use a Gopher client to access a Veronica server, then send Veronica a search request. Veronica servers give you answers in a variety of ways, such as by listing only directories that match your request.

WAIS (Wide Area Information Server) A method for searching databases over the Internet. WAIS was once trumpeted as the next big thing on the Internet, but has not lived up to the promise. Free versions of WAIS servers and clients are hard to use, and few sites run easier-to-use commercial versions. Many Gopher and World Wide Web sites use WAIS to search just within those sites.

wide area network (WAN) A network of computers spread out over a large distance. Some of the connections in a WAN are typically through telephone lines or over satellites. WANs are also often networks of networks, linking local area networks (LANs) into a large single network.

World Wide Web (WWW) An Internet service that lets users retrieve hypertext and graphics from various sites. Often called just "the Web," the World Wide Web has become one of the most popular Internet services in the past two years. In fact, many Internet information providers publish using only the Web.

NetCruiser Software for the Internet

The diskette in the back of this book could be the key to the wonderful world of the Internet. The NetCruiser software, and the Internet services provided by Netcom, are among the most popular on the Internet. If you don't already have an Internet provider and want to get started on the Internet, you're only a few minutes away.

To run the NetCruiser software, you must have a PC running Microsoft Windows, and you need a 9600-baud (or faster) modem.

NetCruiser software works with the Netcom Internet service. Netcom is a nation-wide Internet provider with dial-in locations in over 130 cities across the country. When you install the software, NetCruiser helps you determine the closest location for dialing in. For most people, the call to Netcom is a local call.

Netcom has waived its $25 startup fee for users of the disks bound into this book. If you decide to sign up with Netcom you will only have to pay the monthly usage fee of $19.95. This fee covers up to 40 hours of prime-time service; additional prime-time hours are $2.00 per hour. These fees may have changed by the time you read this, but the software tells you the exact costs before you commit to signing up: Be sure to read all the instructions and announcements during the sign-up process.

Installing the Software

It couldn't be easier:

1. Insert the floppy in your disk drive.

2. From the Windows Program Manager, select the **Run** command from the File menu.

3. Type **A:SETUP** in the Run command's dialog box and click **OK**.

From that point on, the NetCruiser installer program will take over, telling you what it's doing as it copies the files to your hard disk, checking your modem, finding the best phone number for you, and so on. Again, be sure to read each message carefully so that you are aware of all your rights and restrictions in setting up the Netcom account.

You're Always Up to Date

A great feature of NetCruiser is that you can get the latest version of the software automatically with a single command. That way, if the software on the diskette in the back of this book has been updated, you can start your Internet exploration with the very latest NetCruiser software.

The first time you connect to Netcom, choose the **Download New Version** command from the File menu. NetCruiser determines whether or not you have the latest version and, if you don't, downloads each part that needs to be updated. It even tells you its progress each step of the way.

Using the Software

NetCruiser has plenty of online documentation available in the Help menu. However, if you're familiar with even a few Windows programs, you'll have no problem using NetCruiser: It acts just like most other Windows programs. The menus have the normal Windows commands, the windows act the same, and so on. On the off chance that you need technical support, call (408) 983-5970.

Notes

Notes

Notes

_____

_____

_____

_____

_____

_____

_____

_____

_____

_____

_____

_____

_____

_____

_____

_____

_____

_____

Notes

Notes

Notes

Notes

Notes

Notes

_____

_____

_____

_____

_____

_____

_____

_____

_____

_____

_____

_____

_____

_____

_____

_____

_____

_____

Notes

INDEX

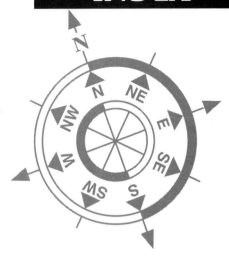

NOTE: Page numbers in italics refer to illustrations or charts.

SYMBOLS

> (greater-than symbol), e-mail replies, *77*
@ (at sign), user addresses, 59–60

A

addresses
  how messages transmit, 47–50
  Internet, 59–61
  TCP/IP (Transmission Control Protocol over Internet Protocol), 42–44
  user, 59–60
advertising
  on Internet, 29
  mail response systems, 99–100
America Online, 25, *26*, 57, 191
analogies, Internet, 11–12
anonymous FTP, 94–98
  Archie and, 158–159
  client software, 98
  defined, 191
Apple Computer, Info-Mac archive, *121*
Archie, 158–159
  defined, *96*, 191

ARPAnet
  defined, 191
  history of Internet, 13–14
  NSFnet and, 17–18
ASCII, defined, 191
AskERIC, K-12 resources, 135, *136*
authentication, defined, 191

B

BBSs (Bulletin Board Systems)
  defined, *119*, 192
  freenets, 51
  Internet connections, 51
  library catalogs, 101
  online services, 26, 58
binary attachments, e-mail, 168
BITNET, defined, 192
business
  commercial sites, 146–149
  e-mail and, 55
  Internet connections for, 54–56
  research, 122–123
buying online, 146–149
  security, 179

C

c shell, UNIX, 66–67, 192
cables for networks, 6
careers and jobs, 144–146
catalogs
  electronic, 54, 147
  library, 100–101
CERT (Computer Emergency Response Team), *68*, 192
channels, IRC (Internet Relay Chat), 106–107
character-based clients, 64–65
chat
  channels, 106–107
  defined, 192
  news and views, 132–135
Chronicle of Higher Education, jobs and careers, *145*

point of presence (POP), defined, *52*, 198
population of Internet, 22–24
  growth statistics, 174–177
ports, defined, 42, 198–199
postal service analogy, Internet, 11–12
PPP (Point-to-Point Protocol), defined, 199
President of the United States, e-mail
      address, 61
privacy. *See* security
Project Gutenberg, *122*
protocols
  file transfer. *See* anonymous FTP
  TCP/IP, 37–44
providers. *See* service providers
publishing
  finger program, 108–110
  on Internet, 54
purchasing online, 146–149, 179

R
Radio, Internet Talk, 107–108, 196
rec hierarchy
  games, 128–130
  travel newsgroups, 142–143
relevance feedback, WAIS databases, 111–112
RFCs (Requests for Comments), 21, 199
routers
  defined, 199
  networks and, 11, 49

S
schools. *See* education
searching, 153–164
  Archie, 158–159
  finger program, 108–110
  for Internet users, 162–164
  Veronica, 155–157
  WAIS databases, 111–112
  Web crawlers, 161
  WWW Virtual Library, 159–160
security
  EFF (Electronic Frontier Foundation), *69*
  financial transactions, 31

finger program, 110
future of Internet, 178–180
  Internet, 68–69
  mailing lists, 92
  PEM (Privacy Enhanced Mail), 164, 179, 198
  searching for people, 162–164
server programs, defined, 199
servers
  clients and, 61–63
  defined, 199
  DNS (Domain Name System), 43–44, 59–61
  FTP. *See* anonymous FTP
  weather, 117
service providers, 25–26, 51–53
  costs of, 51–52
  evaluating, 52–53
  listed, 181–190
services
  levels of Internet, 25
  online, 25–26, 57–58
shareware, defined, 121, 199
sharing connections, 56
shells, defined, *66*, 199
Simtel PC Archives, file repositories, *120*
SLIP/PPP connections
  client software, 65
  defined, 199–200
  Internet, 51, *53*, 58
  World Wide Web, *80*
SMTP (Simple Mail Transport Protocol), 24, *76*
soc hierarchy, newsgroups, 133–134
software
  character-based and graphical clients,
      63–66
  client/server, 61–63, *112*
  network, 6
split messages, 50
sports, 127–132
Sports Index, World Wide Web, *129*
Stanford University, Info-Mac archive, *121*
state government, 138–142
STD (Standards file), defined, 200

IDG Books Worldwide License Agreement

Important — read carefully before opening the software packet(s). This is a legal agreement between you (either an individual or an entity) and IDG Books Worldwide, Inc. (IDG). By opening the accompanying sealed packet(s) containing the software disk(s), you acknowledge that you have read and accept the following IDG License Agreement. If you do not agree and do not want to be bound by the terms of this Agreement, promptly return the book and the unopened software packet(s) to the place you obtained them for a full refund.

1. **License.** This License Agreement (Agreement) permits you to use one copy of the enclosed Software program(s) on a single computer. The Software is in "use" on a computer when it is loaded into temporary memory (i.e., RAM) or installed into permanent memory (e.g., hard disk, CD-ROM, or other storage device) of that computer.

2. **Copyright.** The entire contents of the disk(s) and the compilation of the Software are copyrighted and protected by both United States copyright laws and international treaty provisions. You may only (a) make one copy of the Software for backup or archival purposes, or (b) transfer the Software to a single hard disk, provided that you keep the original for backup or archival purposes. The individual programs on the disk(s) are copyrighted by the authors of each program respectively. Each program has its own use permissions and limitations. To use each program, you must follow the individual requirements and restrictions detailed for each in the Appendix of this Book. Do not use a program if you do not want to follow its Licensing Agreement. None of the material on the disk(s) or listed in this Book may ever be distributed, in original or modified form, for commercial purposes.

3. **Other Restrictions**. You may not rent or lease the Software. You may transfer the Software and user documentation on a permanent basis provided you retain no copies and the recipient agrees to the terms of this Agreement. You may not reverse engineer, decompile, or disassemble the Software except to the extent that the foregoing restriction is expressly prohibited by applicable law. If the Software is an update or has been updated, any transfer must include the most recent update and all prior versions.

4. **Limited Warranty**. IDG warrants that the Software and disk(s) are free from defects in materials and workmanship for a period of sixty (60) days from the date of purchase of this Book. If IDG receives notification within the warranty period of defects in material or workmanship, IDG will replace the defective disk(s). IDG's entire liability and your exclusive remedy shall be limited to replacement of the Software, which is returned to IDG with a copy of your receipt. This Limited Warranty is void if failure of the Software has resulted from accident, abuse, or misapplication. Any replacement Software will be warranted for the remainder of the original warranty period or thirty (30) days, whichever is longer.

5. **No Other Warranties**. To the maximum extent permitted by applicable law, IDG and the author disclaim all other warranties, express or implied, including but not limited to implied warranties of merchantability and fitness for a particular purpose, with respect to the Software, the programs, the source code contained therein and/or the techniques described in this Book. This limited warranty gives you specific legal rights. You may have others which vary from state/jurisdiction to state/jurisdiction.

6. **No Liability For Consequential Damages**. To the extent permitted by applicable law, in no event shall IDG or the author be liable for any damages whatsoever (including without limitation, damages for loss of business profits, business interruption, loss of business information, or any other pecuniary loss) arising out of the use of or inability to use the Book or the Software, even if IDG has been advised of the possibility of such damages. Because some states/jurisdictions do not allow the exclusion or limitation of liability for consequential or incidental damages, the above limitation may not apply to you.

7. **U.S.Government Restricted Rights**. Use, duplication, or disclosure of the Software by the U.S. Government is subject to restrictions stated in paragraph (c) (1) (ii) of the Rights in Technical Data and Computer Software clause of DFARS 252.227-7013, and in subparagraphs (a) through (d) of the Commercial Computer—Restricted Rights clause at FAR 52.227-19, and in similar clauses in the NASA FAR supplement, when applicable.

IDG BOOKS WORLDWIDE REGISTRATION CARD

RETURN THIS REGISTRATION CARD FOR FREE CATALOG

Title of this book: Destination INTERNET & World Wide Web

My overall rating of this book: ❏ Very good [1] ❏ Good [2] ❏ Satisfactory [3] ❏ Fair [4] ❏ Poor [5]

How I first heard about this book:

❏ Found in bookstore; name: [6]

❏ Advertisement: [8]

❏ Word of mouth; heard about book from friend, co-worker, etc.: [10]

❏ Book review: [7]

❏ Catalog: [9]

❏ Other: [11]

What I liked most about this book:

What I would change, add, delete, etc., in future editions of this book:

Other comments:

Number of computer books I purchase in a year: ❏ 1 [12] ❏ 2-5 [13] ❏ 6-10 [14] ❏ More than 10 [15]

I would characterize my computer skills as: ❏ Beginner [16] ❏ Intermediate [17] ❏ Advanced [18] ❏ Professional [19]

I use ❏ DOS [20] ❏ Windows [21] ❏ OS/2 [22] ❏ Unix [23] ❏ Macintosh [24] ❏ Other: [25]_____
(please specify)

I would be interested in new books on the following subjects:
(please check all that apply, and use the spaces provided to identify specific software)

❏ Word processing: [26]

❏ Data bases: [28]

❏ File Utilities: [30]

❏ Networking: [32]

❏ Other: [34]

❏ Spreadsheets: [27]

❏ Desktop publishing: [29]

❏ Money management: [31]

❏ Programming languages: [33]

I use a PC at (please check all that apply): ❏ home [35] ❏ work [36] ❏ school [37] ❏ other: [38] _____

The disks I prefer to use are ❏ 5.25 [39] ❏ 3.5 [40] ❏ other: [41]_____

I have a CD ROM: ❏ yes [42] ❏ no [43]

I plan to buy or upgrade computer hardware this year: ❏ yes [44] ❏ no [45]

I plan to buy or upgrade computer software this year: ❏ yes [46] ❏ no [47]

Name: _____ Business title: [48] _____ Type of Business: [49] _____

Address (❏ home [50] ❏ work [51]/Company name: _____)

Street/Suite# _____

City [52]/State [53]/Zipcode [54]: _____ Country [55] _____

❏ **I liked this book!** You may quote me by name in future IDG Books Worldwide promotional materials.

My daytime phone number is _____

IDG BOOKS
®
THE WORLD OF COMPUTER KNOWLEDGE

❏ **YES!**
Please keep me informed about IDG's World of Computer Knowledge.
Send me the latest IDG Books catalog.